MUST-TRY
CRAFT
BEERS
OF OHIO

MUST-TRY
CRAFT
BEERS
OF OHIO

Rick Armon

OHIO UNIVERSITY PRESS

Athens

Ohio University Press, Athens, Ohio 45701
ohioswallow.com
© 2017 by Ohio University Press

Printed in the United States of America
Ohio University Press books are printed on acid-free paper ∞™
27 26 25 24 23 22 21 20 19 18 17   5 4 3 2 1

Unless otherwise noted, all photographs were provided by the author.

Library of Congress Cataloging-in-Publication Data

Names: Armon, Rick.
Title: 50 must-try craft beers of Ohio / Rick Armon.
Other titles: Craft beers of Ohio | Beers of Ohio
Description: Athens : Ohio University Press, [2017] | Includes
  bibliographical references and index.
Identifiers: LCCN 2017016170| ISBN 9780821422670 (pb : alk. paper) | ISBN
  9780821446003 (pdf)
Subjects: LCSH: Microbreweries—Ohio—Guidebooks. |
  Breweries—Ohio—Guidebooks. | Beer—Ohio.
Classification: LCC TP577 .A688 2017 | DDC 663/.309771—dc23
LC record available at https://lccn.loc.gov/2017016170

ACKNOWLEDGMENTS

Thanks to my wife, Wendy, and son, Knox, for allowing me the time to put this book together. At one point, late in the writing process, four-year-old Knox marched into our home office and demanded that I stop working and go outside and play with him. "You work every day," he complained. Just wait, I thought, your time will come.

Thanks also to Tom Aguero of BrewMinds (BrewMinds.com) and Patrick Woodward of Pat's Pints (patspints.com) who were both helpful with advice on which beers to choose for this book. And, of course, thanks to the brewers and other individuals for taking the time to share their stories with me and to offer recommendations.

CONTENTS

10 Coolest Breweries to Visit

10 Coolest Brewery Names

10 Influential Individuals in the Ohio Craft Beer Industry

10 Ohio Foods Paired with an Ohio Craft Beer

INTRODUCTION

There's never been a better time to be a craft beer drinker in Ohio. Ever. Just head out to any reputable bar or restaurant and check out the beer menu. Or wander down the beer aisle at the grocery store and marvel at the selection. Or stop by the local growler shop that specializes in fresh draft beer. Or better yet, visit your local brewery or breweries and sample at their tasting rooms.

Ohio is overflowing with craft beer diversity today—both from out-of-state breweries distributing here and from the growing number of Ohio breweries opening. Amazingly, 22 of the 25 largest craft breweries in the United States now sell their beer in Ohio, the seventh-most-populous state in the nation. And Ohio, which at the turn of the century had only about 20 craft brewers, boasted *more than 200 in 2017.*

We are a state of beer lovers. We consume about 30.1 gallons per capita each year, or an astounding 321 beers per person. All that drinking contributes mightily to the state economy.

The Beer Institute and National Beer Wholesalers Association estimated in 2017 that the beer industry, including Anheuser-Busch InBev and MillerCoors—both with breweries in Ohio—had a $13 billion impact on the state economy. That's billion with a "b." There are more than 40,000 people employed in the state thanks to the beer industry, according to their *Beer Serves America* report.

Meanwhile, the Brewers Association, the trade group for craft brewers, based in Boulder, Colorado, reported in 2013 that the craft beer industry provided a $1.2 billion bump to the Ohio economy. Those numbers are growing, thanks to breweries opening in record numbers.

The Ohio breweries range from tiny operations that swap out their beers as fast as they are consumed to two of the largest craft brewers in the United States: Boston Beer, which operates a Samuel Adams brewery in Cincinnati, and Great Lakes Brewing in Cleveland.

The craft beer revolution started in Ohio in 1988 when Great Lakes opened a seven-barrel brewpub in Cleveland's Ohio City neighborhood. Ohio's craft beer industry has had its ups and downs since. There was the boom in the 1990s when everyone decided to open a brewpub. They popped up everywhere. Then many places fizzled and went out of business. The problem, in some cases, came from restaurateurs who opened breweries without knowing how to run a successful brewery and in others, from brewers who opened restaurants without knowing how to run a successful restaurant. Perhaps some of the failures could be blamed on beer drinkers themselves for not being fully ready to embrace craft beer.

Ohio started to see another swell in the late 2000s, with much, but not all, of that growth centered in northeast Ohio around Cleveland. Hoppin' Frog Brewery in Akron, Cornerstone Brewing in Berea, Jackie O's Brewery in Athens, Mt. Carmel Brewing in Mt. Carmel, Rivertown Brewing in Lockland, Weasel Boy Brewing in Zanesville, and others all got their start during the decade.

The floodgates opened in the early 2010s. By the beginning of 2012, there were 49 breweries in the state, including Anheuser-Busch and MillerCoors. At that point, there wasn't a single brewery in Dayton or its suburbs. A mere five years later, there were more than 200 statewide—with 15 in the Dayton area. Cincinnati and Columbus also experienced big gains.

But it's not just major Ohio cities enjoying this latest craft beer buzz. Midsized communities such as Newark, Mansfield, Portsmouth, Athens, and Findlay have their own breweries. You can even find them in small towns like Millersburg (pop. 3,070), Heath (pop. 10,389), Lisbon (pop. 2,783), and Port Clinton (pop. 6,047).

It wasn't always like this. *Wait; scratch that.* It actually was like this before Prohibition. Back then every town had a brewery or two. But the rise of Anheuser-Busch and Miller, thanks in part to ingenious national advertising, blew away all those regional breweries in Ohio. They're back now, in the form of craft operations.

There are plenty of reasons behind the recent explosion. For starters, people are drinking more craft beer, and bars, restaurants, and grocery stores are taking notice and offering more brands. The movement to shop local and eat local didn't hurt, either.

Ohio also became much more beer friendly. State legislators amended outdated laws, making it easier for craft brewers to open and flourish here.

One of the biggest changes was, at least in the eyes of brewers, a no-brainer. Before 2012, brewers weren't allowed to serve their beer at their businesses. *Wait; scratch that, too.* Serving beer was allowed, but only if the brewers bought a second state license for $3,906. And that license had to be renewed every year.

In other words, if a brewery wanted to open a tasting room, it had to pay $3,906 a year for a brewing license and another $3,906 to serve its beer. Without that second license, a brewery could offer a tour but could not give samples at the tour's end. That kept many breweries closed and off limits to their fans. The funny thing was that wineries had no such restriction. They could make their wine and sell it on the premises without purchasing a separate, costly license.

In 2012, the law changed, and brewers started opening tasting rooms left and right. The change allowed brewers to give people the chance to literally drink in the experience of being at a brewery.

"To those who have come for our tours, our saving grace has always been the depth of the explanation of our brewing," former Mt. Carmel assistant brewer Patrick Clark told me at the time the law took effect. "But let's be honest—tasting is the most important part of the process."

Not only did the change create a new marketing tool for the brands, it also provided an influx of cash. Beer drinkers were now coming to the breweries and slapping down money to taste the freshest beer available instead of buying it at a bar, restaurant, or store. They were getting it at the source.

This allowed some new brewers, especially those interested in opening nanobreweries, to get into the craft brewing industry while keeping their day jobs. They could brew during the week and open their breweries on the weekends as they got their businesses off the ground. The money generated by sales at their tasting rooms kept the breweries afloat.

Then in 2013, the state made things even easier. It created a new brewing license for craft brewers. Instead of buying a $3,906 A1 license, any brewer that produced less than 30 million gallons a year—only Anheuser-Busch and MillerCoors exceed that amount here—could buy an A1C license for $1,000. Just like that, it was $2,906 less expensive to open a brewery in Ohio.

But I'm getting off track. This book isn't intended to be a history lesson. It's about showcasing award-winning, tasty, and unusual Ohio-made beers. Let's get this out of the way upfront. The beers showcased here are not necessarily the best in the Buckeye State. The best beer is whatever you think it is.

If that's Thirsty Dog Raspberry Ale, so be it. If it's Triple Digit Chickow!, so be it. If it's Columbus Bodhi, so be it. Even if it's Bud Light, so be it. You get the picture?

There is no way to compile an objective list of the "best" beers when everyone's best will vary. That's why this book is entitled *50 Must-Try Craft Beers of Ohio*. The 50 likely include some of your favorites. Then again, maybe they don't. But I hope this list will spark debate and, perhaps, give you a reason to sample something you have never tried before.

With hundreds upon hundreds of Ohio-made beers to choose from, it wasn't easy determining which brews should make the cut.

Sure, picking some was easy. A few have won numerous awards at major beer competitions and earned a spot on pedigree alone. As of this writing, Fat Head's Head Hunter IPA has taken home four medals at the Great American Beer Festival and the World Beer Cup. It has also won gold at the West Coast IPA Festival—the first East Coast beer to do so. That's not bad for a brewery that opened in 2009. Head Hunter is considered one of the best IPAs in the country. How could it not be represented here?

Then there's Great Lakes Christmas Ale. In northeast Ohio, it has an over-the-top, cult-like following. You know those people who do nothing but talk about their favorite television shows. Christmas Ale is like that for them. It is the best holiday beer ever, hands-down. No debate allowed. The brewery releases the beer on draft with plenty of fanfare, even including a Santa Claus. The first day it goes on sale at the brewery gift shop, you can watch fan after fan leave with cases in hand.

Meanwhile, there's Elevator Ghost Scorpion Lager. It has won no awards. But the first batch—made for the Fiery Foods Festival in Columbus—was so insanely hot, people vomited after drinking it. Yes, that's right. People who like insanely hot foods threw up. How could any beer adventurer not want to sample it? I did. And I immediately started drinking milk because it burned all the way down my throat into my stomach.

So let's see. An award-winning beer, a popular beer, and an unusual beer—there are at least three reasons why a beer could make this list of 50 must-try brews.

To qualify, a beer has to be available either year-round or on a seasonal basis. In other words, you, the reader, have to be able to buy it. One-offs, those brews made only for special occasions or events, weren't considered.

When I first started discussing this idea, I thought it would be difficult to come up with 50 beers. Boy, was I wrong. As a newspaper reporter who has covered the beer industry for more than a decade and a beer blogger who has traveled the state tasting all that Ohio has to offer, I compiled an initial list of 76 beers. But that was my working list *before* I visited the new breweries that have opened in recent years, *before* I reached out to brewers and others I respect to get their opinions, and *before* I realized that there were way too many India pale ales and stouts on my list.

Self-doubt crept into my head early. How could I possibly pare the Ohio craft beer industry to just 50? How could I leave out this beer or that beer? What did I get myself into? Then, I would sit at a brewery, sampler in hand. I would recall how exhilarating it is to talk with brewers about the beer itself, to see their absolute passion for what I was sipping. For me, beer is about more than just the liquid. It's also about the personalities and stories behind each brand. That's what I want to share with you in this book.

I've also included other beers to try if you enjoy the one showcased.

Now, if I had limited this book to 50 beers, it would be pretty short. And, as I've mentioned, beer is about more than the liquid for me.

So I've included four other chapters. I recommend 10 cool breweries to visit and have a beer. There's a chapter telling the stories behind the 10 coolest brewery names. There are profiles of 10 influential people in the Ohio craft beer industry. And I describe 10 quintessential Ohio foods and recommend a beer to drink with each one.

One last word of warning—I started researching this book in 2014. There has been an explosion in not only the number of breweries that have opened in Ohio but also the number of beers produced.

It hasn't been easy trying to keep track of everything new. The task, as my editor Ricky Huard kept reminding me, was a "moving target." It indeed was. One beer originally to be featured in the book was scrapped at the last minute because the brewery closed. In another case, a brewery changed its name. Then, there were all the breweries that decided to redesign their beer labels after I had taken photos. And, as happens all too frequently in the craft beer industry, brewers came and went while I was writing and rewriting.

Trying to keep on top of it all was both a fun and frustrating process. Cheers!

MUST-TRY
**CRAFT
BEERS**
OF OHIO

Albino Stout

Butcher and the Brewer | www.butcherandthebrewer.com

Butcher and the Brewer
2043 E. Fourth St.
Cleveland, Ohio 44115
(216) 331-0805

First brewed: 2014
Style: Other/specialty
Alcohol content: 5.4 percent
IBUs: 15
Available: Year-round on draft

IF YOU LIKE THIS BEER, here are five other Ohio craft coffee beers to try:

- Wolf's Ridge Clear Sky Daybreak
- Willoughby Kaffee Kolsch
- Woodburn Han Solo
- Jackie O's Cool Beans
- Lineage Oscura Obscura

Albino Stout

www.butcherandthebrewer.com | Butcher and the Brewer

FORMER BUTCHER AND THE BREWER brewmaster Eric Anderson likes to have fun and mess with people—especially beer drinkers. He decided to call his raspberry wheat Framboyzee (pronounced fram-BOY-zee) because, over the years, he got tired of people mispronouncing framboise (pronounced fra-BWAZ). He also opted to call his German hefeweizen Hasselhefe because Germans love them some David Hasselhoff of *Baywatch* fame.

But those beers pale in comparison to the Butcher and the Brewer's Albino Stout, a brew so offbeat that it messes with your senses. It's straw in color but features a robust coffee aroma and flavor. In other words, it's a light-colored beer that tastes like a dark beer.

"If you drink it with your eyes closed, you'd think you're drinking a dark beer," Anderson says while sitting at the brewpub's bar. "I just think it's funny. It's playful."

The recipe stemmed from his frustration with beer drinkers who say they don't like dark beer. Anderson wanted to poke fun at them and prove that a beer's color doesn't define its flavor.

The reactions after the first sniff and sip are precious. Many don't know what to say. Anderson had planned to make Albino Stout just once. But the beer sold so well that it made its way into the brewery's regular lineup.

"The one rule I live by is brew what you want to drink," Anderson says. "That's how I do it. What's the point of copying everybody else? Every recipe I make starts from the ground up. I don't clone Sierra Nevada and then try to tweak it like I want it. Everything starts from the bottom. It's like being a chef."

AlpenGlow

Fat Head's Brewery | www.fatheadsbeer.com

Fat Head's Brewery

Production brewery/tasting room:
17450 Engle Lake Drive
Middleburg Heights, Ohio 44130*
(216) 898-0242

Brewpub:
24581 Lorain Road
North Olmsted, Ohio 44070
(440) 801-1001

First brewed: 2010
Style: Weizenbock
Alcohol content: 8.5 percent
IBUs: 22
Awards: Gold medals in 2014 and 2016 and a silver medal in 2012 at the Great American Beer Festival
Available: Year-round, but availability varies

IF YOU LIKE THIS BEER, here are five other Ohio craft beers to try:

- Great Lakes Glockenspiel
- Willoughby St. Otto
- Market Garden Big Wheat
- Blank Slate Tank Bottoms
- Christian Moerlein Emancipator Doppelbock

*Opening November 2017

AlpenGlow

www.fatheadsbeer.com | Fat Head's Brewery

QUICK, NAME THE FAT HEAD'S BEER that has been the biggest winner at the Great American Beer Festival. Be honest. Your answer was Hop JuJu (two golds and a bronze) or Head Hunter (a silver and a bronze), wasn't it? Well, both of those are great guesses, given the brewery's reputation for hoppy beers, but wrong—at least as of 2016.

AlpenGlow, a weizenbock, has taken home two gold medals and a silver.

"Has it won three times?" Fat Head's co-owner and brewer Matt Cole says with a laugh. "I knew it was at least twice but I didn't know it was three times. It's a damn good beer."

Weizenbocks are strong, dark Bavarian wheat beers. AlpenGlow was inspired by Schneider Weisse Aventinus, Pennsylvania Brewing Co.'s weizenbock, and a doppelbock that Cole made while working at Baltimore Brewing Co. He also gives heavy credit to Fat Head's brewpub brewer Mike Zoscak for rounding the beer into award-winning shape.

Fat Head's uses a variety of malts, including a bitter chocolate malt and Munich malt, which help mask the higher alcohol level.

"We like it to have a rich malt profile but also a lot of character of dried fruit and some subdued chocolate," Cole says. "It's really modeled after the classic Bavarian weizenbock beers."

The real magic, though, happens when the brewery ferments AlpenGlow with a blend of German yeast strains. The blending adds a layer of complexity to the flavor and provides the banana, bubblegum, and clove characteristics that wheat beer fans crave. Fat Head's also uses a process called free rise fermentation, allowing AlpenGlow to ferment as the temperature rises naturally over a period of time.

"It's probably one of the most complex beers that we make," Cole says. "We have a lot of pretty complicated beers. But it's one of those beers that there are a lot of extra steps we do in the process."

As for the name, AlpenGlow stems from a phenomenon experienced by many skiers. "When the sun sets on the backside of a mountain, you get this little bit of a glow, and it has these really deep mahogany ruby highlights," Cole says. "It's a really pretty beer."

Anastasia Russian Imperial Stout

Weasel Boy Brewing Co. | www.weaselboybrewing.com

Weasel Boy Brewing Co.
126 Muskingum Ave.
Zanesville, Ohio 43701
(740) 455-3767

First brewed: 2007

Style: Russian imperial stout

Alcohol content: 8 percent

IBUs: 68

Awards: Gold medal in 2012 and bronze medal in 2010 at the Great American Beer Festival

Available: November through March on draft

IF YOU LIKE THIS BEER, here are five other Ohio craft beers to try:

- Barley's Alexander's Russian Imperial Stout
- Jackie O's Dark Apparition
- Thirsty Dog Siberian Night Imperial Stout
- MadTree Axis Mundi
- Rhinegeist Ink

Anastasia Russian Imperial Stout

www.weaselboybrewing.com | Weasel Boy Brewing Co.

ANASTASIA RUSSIAN IMPERIAL STOUT made its professional debut in 2007, but it had been around long before then. Owner and brewer Jay Wince, a fan of imperial stouts, made it as a homebrew in 2001, the first beer recipe that he ever designed on his own. (Two years later, the beer won an annual homebrew competition at Barley's Brewing.)

Influenced by Bell's Expedition, Wince set out to create a British-style imperial stout that was heavier on the malt flavor and lower in alcohol content.

"I wanted a fairly full-bodied, rich beer for sipping, no matter what temperature," he says. "Most people really like those in the cold weather. It's something to throw in a snifter and really enjoy."

He certainly succeeded in producing an enjoyable brew. The beer is a two-time winner at the Great American Beer Festival, taking home a gold and a bronze. Wince, who launched the Weasel Boy production brewery and tasting room in 2007 with his wife, Lori, says it's especially satisfying to win twice.

Anastasia, which is available only on draft, also comes in a version aged in bourbon barrels. In 2014, Weasel Boy had fun by tossing it in a Cabernet barrel.

Anyone familiar with Weasel Boy knows that its beers feature some sort of weasel-related name. That's thanks to the Winces' love of the animals. Anastasia, obviously, is the anomaly.

The name dates back to the beer's homebrew days, when Jay was searching for a Russian-related name. There were plenty of Alexanders, a reference to various Russian tsars. He opted for Anastasia, the daughter of the last tsar, Nicholas II, who was executed along with his family in 1918. The homebrew picked up numerous medals at national competitions, so Wince saw no reason to change the name when Weasel Boy opened.

As for his original homebrewed batch of Anastasia, Wince still has two bottles aging. He's hoping to crack them open when celebrating future Great American Beer Festival wins.

Barley's Scottish Ale

Barley's Brewing Co. | www.barleysbrewing.com

Barley's Brewing Co.
467 N. High St.
Columbus, Ohio 43215
(614) 228-2537

First brewed: 1993
Style: Scotch ale
Alcohol content: 6.6 percent
IBUs: 14
Available: Year-round on draft

IF YOU LIKE THIS BEER, here are five other Ohio craft beers to try:

- Smokehouse MacLenny's Scottish Ale
- Millersburg Doc's Scotch Ale
- Thirsty Dog Twisted Kilt Scottish Export Ale
- Market Garden Wallace Tavern Scotch Ale
- Fifty West Going Plaid

Barley's Scottish Ale

www.barleysbrewing.com | Barley's Brewing Co.

BARLEY'S HEAD BREWER Angelo Signorino Jr. still remembers his boss's response when he mentioned his plan to create a Scottish ale. Signorino, then the assistant brewer, wanted to make a beer similar to MacAndrew's Scotch Ale from Scotland.

To do so, he was going to fire up the gas burners to preheat the brew kettle and scorch the wort for a full half-hour, caramelizing it and getting the strongest malt flavor possible. The bottom of the brew kettle at Barley's just happens to be flatter than most, making it difficult to clean but perfect for scorching wort evenly.

Former head brewer Scott Francis, though, initially was a little skeptical about the process. "Do you know how much that brew kettle costs?" he asked at the time.

Signorino reassured him that the plan was to keep the bottom of the kettle covered in water right up until sending in the wort, so the long scorch wasn't going to damage the equipment. At least he didn't think it would.

The beer—made with pale malts, British carapils, and a little bit of wheat—turned out to be a winner. Since that first batch in late 1993, it has always been on draft and has become Barley's flagship beer. For years, the ale was called MacLenny's Scottish Ale, but it was renamed Barley's Scottish Ale in 2015. All the caramel flavor and color comes from that scorching, which caramelizes the sugars in a way similar to the process of making crème brûlée.

Signorino has never varied that time-consuming, half-hour process.

"After all these years, you look for ways to shave minutes off the day, get home to your family sooner, but it's not a compromise that we'll make with the Scottish," he says. "We'll continue to scorch it for that full half an hour because the results make it worthwhile."

For years, Signorino also brewed at the nearby Smokehouse Brewing Company in Columbus and made a Scottish ale there. But it just wasn't the same, given the different makeup of the brew kettle.

"This brewery's version is one of a kind for sure," Signorino says.

Berliner Weisse

Jackie O's Brewery | www.jackieos.com

Jackie O's Brewery

Production brewery/tasting room:
25 Campbell St.
Athens, Ohio 45701
(740) 447-9063

Brewpub:
24 W. Union St.
Athens, Ohio 45701
(740) 592-9686

First brewed: 2011
Style: Berliner weisse
Alcohol content: 5 percent
IBUs: 14
Available: Year-round

IF YOU LIKE THIS BEER, here are five other Ohio craft beers to try:

- Thirsty Dog Berliner Weisse
- Rivertown Divergent
- Actual Curiosus
- Lineage Weekend at Bernice's
- Urban Artifact Finn

Berliner Weisse

www.jackieos.com | Jackie O's Brewery

JACKIE O'S PUTS its own spin on the Berliner weisse style, a sour wheat beer. The low-alcohol cloudy brew dates back to the sixteenth century and originated in northern Germany, but plenty of domestic craft brewers have opted to create their own versions as more American beer drinkers embrace sours.

Known for his love of experimentation, brewmaster Brad Clark started playing around with sours in 2008. At first he made a few brown ales and golden ales. But he really got intrigued with the style after reading about sherry and the solera production method. And that solera approach is what separates Jackie O's Berliner Weisse from other sours.

The solera technique involves pulling some of the liquid out of the brewing vessel, but leaving some of it behind. The vessel is never really emptied, meaning the new is always blended with the old.

"Essentially part of the original batch is still in there," Clark says. "You have this kombucha-esque, mother-culture-type thing. I got kind of infatuated with that."

He had been drinking some Berliner weisse brews at the time and figured he could make his own version using the solera method. To produce his Berliner Weisse, Clark made several different batches—one using lactobacillus and others with strains of brettanomyces—and blended them together. He uses no brewing yeast, and he has never cleaned the three-and-one-half-barrel grundy tanks that hold the Berliner Weisse, creating a truly unique beer that features a distinctly funky and lemon character.

"I believe, and I'm biased obviously, each time that it comes out, it tastes better," Clark says.

As expected, Clark has some fun with his Berliner Weisse and has produced plenty of varieties through the years. Depending on how he's feeling at the time, you might find a peach version—or a blueberry, or even a kumquat.

Blackout Stout

Great Lakes Brewing Co. | www.greatlakesbrewing.com

Great Lakes Brewing Co.
2516 Market Ave.
Cleveland, Ohio 44113
(216) 771-4404

First brewed: 2003
Style: Imperial stout
Alcohol content: 9 percent
IBUs: 50
Awards: Gold medal in 2006 and bronze in 2008 at the World Beer Cup
Available: In November on draft and in bottles

IF YOU LIKE THIS BEER, here are five other Ohio craft beers to try:

- Thirsty Dog Siberian Night
- Hoof Hearted Voltan
- Willoughby B.D.A.
- Fifty West Ghost of Imogene
- Jackie O's Dark Apparition

Blackout Stout

Great Lakes Brewing Co. | www.greatlakesbrewing.com

GREAT LAKES BLACKOUT STOUT was born out of an actual blackout. Seriously.

It was August 14, 2003, when the largest power outage in US history rolled across the Midwest and Northeast, affecting an estimated 50 million people from Ohio to New York to Ontario, Canada.

In Cleveland, folks descended in droves on Great Lakes Brewing. Cofounder Pat Conway theorizes that they figured, without power, the brewery couldn't keep its beer cold. Better get it before it warms up.

Those who showed up that day got a special treat. Without power, the cash registers didn't work. So Conway remembers just giving away free beer.

He recalls sitting in the open beer garden next door—the space has since been enclosed—with hundreds of others as they looked up through the black of night and stared at the stars.

"That's how the world had been for millions of years up until the early part of the twentieth century," Conway says. "Everybody saw stars. Now, we saw it for a brief night. It was spectacular."

Meanwhile, Conway's brother and cofounder, Dan, was driving home on Lorain Avenue, with every traffic light going out just as he passed by. It was a comical moment.

"I thought, 'Am I doing this?'" he says.

The memories were so unforgettable that Great Lakes designed Blackout Stout, a powerful, black-as-night Russian imperial stout that's served in a snifter. The beer, available in four-packs and on draft, has become one of the brewery's highest-rated beers by RateBeer and BeerAdvocate.

Blackout Stout, which also comes in a barrel-aged version, has a cult following, and the brewery holds a launch party for its release every year.

The 2014 party was held, appropriately, in the dark.

Bleeding Buckeye Red Ale

Elevator Brewing Co. | www.elevatorbrewery.com

Elevator Brewing Co.

Brewery & Draught Haus:
161 N. High St.
Columbus, Ohio 43215
(614) 228-0500

Taproom:
165 N. Fourth St.
Columbus, Ohio 43215
(614) 679-2337

First brewed: 2004
Style: Red ale
Alcohol content: 5.7 percent
IBUs: 27
Available: Year-round on draft and in bottles

IF YOU LIKE THIS BEER, here are five other Ohio craft beers to try:

- Moeller Brew Barn Wally Post Red
- Thirsty Dog Irish Setter Red Ale
- R. Shea Rubber City Red
- Buckeye Redhead
- Great Lakes Rally Drum Red Ale

Bleeding Buckeye Red Ale

www.elevatorbrewery.com | Elevator Brewing Co.

THE OWNER of Elevator Brewing, Dick Stevens, thought it would be a great idea to brew a beer that would capitalize on the passion that Columbus has for Ohio State University football. The Buckeyes rule the local sports landscape, so the community nearly shuts down on game days, with people either heading to watch the game live at Ohio Stadium or planting themselves in front of their televisions.

The brewery designed an approachable malty beer and dubbed it Bleeding Buckeye Red Ale. The name plays on the fact that Ohio State fans bleed scarlet and gray.

On the label, Stevens put a black-and-white picture of people illustrating the famous O-H-I-O—a sort of shadow puppet image. There was one problem. Ohio State didn't approve, thinking the design encroached on its brand. Elevator received a cease-and-desist order from the university.

Six thousand dollars later—thanks to the involvement of law firms—the brewery had a new label.

"I had a hard time getting any law firm to work for me because, if they had done any work for OSU, it was a conflict of interest," Stevens says. "Every little change had to be sent over there to be approved."

The label has been redesigned a couple of times since. The first design used a cartoon of a group of fans cheering on their favorite team and the Ohio State colors —black, scarlet, and gray. Now the label features a photograph of cheering fans—all wearing the Ohio State colors, of course—piling out of a red van.

And, without a doubt, Bleeding Buckeye sells the best during football season.

Blood Thirst Wheat

Barley's Brewing Co. | www.barleysbrewing.com

Barley's Brewing Co.
467 N. High St.
Columbus, Ohio 43215
(614) 228-2537

First brewed: 2010
Style: Fruit beer
Alcohol content: 5 percent
IBUs: 2.9
Available: Year-round on draft

IF YOU LIKE THIS BEER, here are five other Ohio craft beers to try:

- Old Firehouse Maltese Cross
- MadTree Blood Orange PsycHOPathy
- Maumee Bay Blood Orange Imperial Witbier
- Thirsty Dog Raspberry Ale
- Rivertown Blueberry Lager

Blood Thirst Wheat

www.barleysbrewing.com | Barley's Brewing Co.

EACH YEAR, Barley's Brewing hosts a homebrew competition. A small batch of the winning beer is brewed for release at the brewpub the following year for all to enjoy. Usually, the beer is never heard from again.

But all that changed in 2009, the year of the 14th annual competition. Homebrewer Lloyd Cicetti devised a Bavarian wheat ale, using blood oranges. The beer was a hit when it went on tap in 2010. It proved to be so popular that Barley's head brewer Angelo Signorino Jr. opted to make it again—and again, and again.

Cicetti didn't have a detailed recipe written down. There was no starting gravity, for example, to work from, so Signorino improvised. The brewery zests blood oranges by hand and uses blood orange puree. The beer, wonderfully cloudy with a hint of crimson color, initially was available only during the summer. But it kept selling so well that Barley's opted to start brewing it year-round in late 2014.

So what explains its popularity? "It is so accessible," Signorino says. "It's fruity, but it's not like a fruit beer. And one of the things that I'm really proud of is that it's not flavoring. It's really orange puree and real orange zest. I think it shows in the beer."

Blood Thirst Wheat also is special to Signorino because it recognizes the creativity of homebrewers.

"When I started brewing at home in 1991 and here in 1992, I wouldn't have considered that beer," he says with a laugh. "What do you mean? A Bavarian wheat beer with blood oranges? That's not beer. But people love it. It's remarkably refreshing and satisfying."

Blood Thirst Wheat is the only winning beer from the homebrew competition that has gone on to become a regular at Barley's.

Bodhi

Columbus Brewing Co. | www.columbusbrewing.com

Columbus Brewing Co.
2555 Harrison Road
Columbus, Ohio 43204
(614) 224-3626

First brewed: 2009
Style: Double India pale ale
Alcohol content: 8.5 percent
IBUs: Low 90s
Awards: Bronze medal at the 2014 Great American Beer Festival
Available: Year-round on draft and in bottles

IF YOU LIKE THIS BEER, here are five other Ohio craft brews to try:

- Rhinegeist Saber Tooth Tiger
- Great Lakes Chillwave
- Homestead 3 MC's
- Hoppin' Frog Hop Dam Triple IPA
- Hoof Hearted Dragonsaddle

Bodhi

www.columbusbrewing.com | Columbus Brewing Co.

COLUMBUS BREWING owner and brewer Eric Bean had just designed his latest beer, an aggressive India pale ale using Citra hops, and he wanted a hip name for it. He read somewhere that consumers gravitated toward beers with fun names.

But when he looked at the names of some of the early Columbus brands... well, they seemed pretty bland. Pale Ale? IPA? It can't get more mundane than that.

"I was looking for a name that sounded cool," Bean says. "All other brewers have cool names. Why don't we have any?"

He chose Bodhi. Now here's where things get interesting. Bean, who has a reputation for producing some of the state's best hoppy brews, doesn't want to reveal why he chose Bodhi, preferring to keep a little mystery behind the name. Of course, there are a few well-known possible inspirations that he freely acknowledges.

For starters, legend has it that Buddha was sitting under a Bodhi tree when he achieved enlightenment. Bodhi is also Sanskrit for enlightenment. Or maybe the name is just paying homage to the kick-ass Bodhi character played by Patrick Swayze in the film *Point Break*.

Whatever the real story, the beer is delicious, and Columbus fans can't get enough of it. For years, the beer was available only on draft. Bean was hounded all the time about when Bodhi would be in bottles. That finally happened in 2016, when Columbus moved to a larger location and upgraded its brewing system.

"We definitely have a philosophy around our hoppy beers," Bean says. "I don't like bitter hoppy beers. I think that's the beauty of Bodhi. It's so approachable ... But it's not that it's so soft that the super high-end bitter freak isn't attracted to it, too. That beer is designed for a pretty broad audience."

B.O.R.I.S. the Crusher

Hoppin' Frog Brewery | www.hoppinfrog.com

Hoppin' Frog Brewery
1680 E. Waterloo Road
Akron, Ohio 44306
(330) 352-4578

First brewed: 2006

Style: Imperial stout

Alcohol content: 9.4 percent

IBUs: 60

Awards: Gold medals in 2008 and 2011 at the Great American Beer Festival (The barrel-aged version also has won medals.)

Available: Year-round on draft and in bottles

IF YOU LIKE THIS BEER, here are five other Ohio craft beers to try:

- Seventh Son Oublitte
- Actual Fat Julian
- Hoppin' Frog D.O.R.I.S. the Destroyer
- Weasel Boy Anastasia Russian Imperial Stout
- Royal Docks Vlad the Impaler

B.O.R.I.S. the Crusher

www.hoppinfrog.com | Hoppin' Frog Brewery

B.R.I.S. doesn't exactly paint a picture of a strong, bold brew. The mind wanders to other . . . well, we won't go there. But that's how B.O.R.I.S. the Crusher Oatmeal-Imperial Stout began. Hoppin' Frog Brewery owner and brewer Fred Karm, as a homebrewer, created a big, hearty Russian imperial stout after sampling one at the former Liberty Street Brewing in Akron. Karm knew that an R.I.S. would be part of his lineup when he eventually opened his own brewery.

He dubbed his homebrew "bodacious"—thus the B. But it wasn't until he added oatmeal when he started Hoppin' Frog that Bodacious Oatmeal Russian Imperial Stout, or B.O.R.I.S. for short, was born.

"The oatmeal was a natural additive to that beer to add more body and flavor," Karm says. He also knew that oatmeal could help with marketing, figuring he wanted to attract the same beer drinkers who enjoy the well-known Samuel Smith Oatmeal Stout.

He recalled his first Russian imperial stout homebrew as insane and thick.

"When I started Hoppin' Frog, I wanted to remake those homebrews that make people say 'Oh, my God,'" he says. "The ones you would write home about. The ones you would covet, not wanting to drink the last one. Those are the beers that I wanted to make here. That bodacious Russian imperial stout was perfect."

B.O.R.I.S. went on to win gold medals at the Great American Beer Festival in 2008 and 2011. It also is the award-winning beer that keeps on giving.

Karm has released many barrel-aged versions of B.O.R.I.S., winning a gold medal at the 2012 World Beer Cup and a bronze at the 2013 Great American Beer Festival. He even created D.O.R.I.S. the Destroyer Double Imperial Stout, the hoppier cousin to B.O.R.I.S.

"From day one, my staff felt [B.O.R.I.S.] was a winner, and my longest employee said you're going to win a gold with this," Karm says. "And we did. I couldn't frickin' believe it. From day one, it tasted so good I never messed with the recipe—never, ever. It's one of those recipes that people lock up in safes. Oh yeah, we locked it up. That's a recipe I think a lot of people want to get their hands on."

Bumble Berry

Fat Head's Brewery | www.fatheadsbeer.com

Fat Head's Brewery

Production brewery/tasting room:
17450 Engle Lake Drive
Middleburg Heights, Ohio 44130*
(216) 898-0242

Brewpub:
24581 Lorain Road
North Olmsted, Ohio 44070
(440) 801-1001

First brewed: 2009

Style: Fruit beer

Alcohol content: 5.3 percent

IBUs: 13

Awards: Won the Brewing News Global Warming Open in 2010

Available: Year-round on draft and in bottles

IF YOU LIKE THIS BEER, here are five other Ohio craft beers to try:

- Rivertown Blueberry Lager
- Rocky River Blueberry Ale
- Thirsty Dog Raspberry Ale
- Willoughby Railway Razz
- Jackie O's Razz Wheat

*Opening November 2017

Bumble Berry

www.fatheadsbeer.com | Fat Head's Brewery

FAT HEAD'S BREWERY has built its reputation with hoppy beers like Head Hunter IPA and Hop JuJu. But every brewery needs that bread-and-butter beer that appeals to a mass audience and sells like crazy.

For Fat Head's, that's Bumble Berry, an ale that features honey and blueberries. The beer, one of the brewery's original recipes, is served at the brewpub with blueberries floating in the glass.

Fruit beers aren't exactly the manliest or the most-sought-after style by craft beer geeks. But co-owner and brewer Matt Cole is far from embarrassed that Bumble Berry has turned into the brewery's best seller. In fact, the brewpub goes through a barrel a day; the brew represents an amazing 20 percent of all the beer consumed at the restaurant.

"I actually got some pushback from some of our partners that that was going to be one of the beers that we were going to start out with," Cole says. "I'm kind of proud of its success, to be honest with you."

The inspiration for Bumble Berry dates back to a trip to Boston and a visit to Boston Beer Works, where Cole was introduced to Bunker Hill Blueebery. The flavor worked, and the beer was refreshing. He figured he would make his own blueberry, eschewing the usual raspberry.

"The nose is great, and the flavor is not offensively sweet," Cole says. "We work hard to get this kind of toasted dryness in the beer that gives it a drinkability. . . . You need one of those beers in your portfolio. It helps pay the bills."

Carillon Porter

Carillon Brewing Co. | www.carillonbrewingco.org

Carillon Brewing Co.
1000 Carillon Blvd.
Dayton, Ohio 45409
(937) 910-0722

First brewed: 2014
Style: Porter
Alcohol content: 6.1 percent
IBUs: Unknown
Available: Year-round on draft

IF YOU LIKE THIS BEER . . . well, good luck finding other porters from the 1800s. But here are five other Ohio craft porters to try:

- Temperance Row 40-Ton Porter
- Old Firehouse Probie
- Restoration Brew Worx Rush Porter
- Yellow Springs Porter
- Lockport Lockporter

Carillon Porter

www.carillonbrewingco.org | Carillon Brewing Co.

CARILLON BREWING makes their porter the old-fashioned way—the *real* old-fashioned way. The brewery, which is part of the Carillon Historical Park in Dayton, was built to replicate brewing from the 1850s, with a small wood-fired, gravity-fed brewhouse that produces only 1.9 barrels of beer at a time.

If the sight of brewers doing their work in period costume isn't a dead giveaway that this isn't your typical brewpub, the roaring fire used to heat the kettle, the volunteers grinding grain by hand, and the ropes and pulleys used to carry ingredients to the top of the two-story brick brewing system should be.

The porter, simply named Porter, is one of the brewery's key beers, along with its Coriander Ale. Befitting Carillon's mission, the brewing process and beer are used to educate rather than intoxicate. All the work is done within plain view of restaurant and bar customers, and the workers are more than happy to talk about the historical brewing process.

"Porters were the young folks who carried and curried things, and they didn't have enough money to afford a strong ale or a strong stout but were tired of drinking a small ale all day long," former brewmaster Tanya Brock says about the history of the style.

Brewers created porter for them and then, recognizing how popular the style became, started brewing it all the time. Carillon didn't design its own porter. Instead, it pulled the recipe from an 1862 Cincinnati cookbook that was written for brewers.

The beer is lighter in body and flavor than modern porters. That has caused more than a few craft beer drinkers to question whether it's a true porter. But again, this is beer as it tasted in the 1800s.

Brock doesn't even know where the beer ranks in terms of IBUs. Then again, why would she? Brewers back in the 1800s didn't focus on that statistic.

Brock smiles when asked how difficult it is to make the beer. It's not an easy process. Two days before making the porter, volunteers hand-roast the heirloom six-row barley, pouring a pound at a time into a skillet and stirring it. The brew day itself lasts anywhere from 12 to 15 hours.

"This is not profitable by any means," Brock says.

Chickow!

Triple Digit Brewing Co. | www.tripledigitbrewing.com

Triple Digit Brewing Co.
1621 Dana Ave.
Cincinnati, Ohio 45207
(513) 731-1130

First brewed: 2012

Style: Brown ale

Alcohol content: 10 percent

IBUs: 28

Awards: The barrel-aged version of Chickow! won the best of show at the 2016 Festival of Barrel and Wood-Aged Beers (FoBAB) in Chicago and a silver medal at the event in 2015

Available: Year-round on draft and in bottles

IF YOU LIKE THIS BEER . . . well, there aren't many other hazelnut brews around. Here are five other darker Ohio craft beers to try:

- Thirsty Dog Rise of the Mayan Dog
- Mt. Carmel Coffee Brown Ale
- Seventh Son Mr. Owl Double India Brown
- Buckeye Warm Fuzzy
- Fat Head's Shakedown

Chickow!

www.tripledigitbrewing.com | Triple Digit Brewing Co.

CHICKOW! WAS never meant to be a year-round beer. Heck, it was never meant to be brewed more than once. Former head brewer Kevin Moreland decided to create the imperial brown ale made with hazelnuts for Listermann's inaugural Oktoberfest, which featured Cincinnati's craft brewers.

The strong hazelnut flavor, combined with its high gravity, proved to be an overwhelming hit with beer geeks and novices alike. But perhaps the complex malt base is the most inviting, with people picking up vanilla, caramel, and chocolate flavors and a little heat from the alcohol.

"It caught a lot of people off guard," says Patrick Gilroy, who worked the festival as a volunteer and later served as head brewer. "It was pretty obvious it was unique and you couldn't compare it to anything."

A few months later, after word spread about this tasty and unusual brew, Triple Digit couldn't make enough of it. Chickow! serves as the brewery's flagship.

Gilroy also realized that Chickow! is quite the versatile beer, as it meshes well with all kinds of infusions. The brewery has released a seemingly endless number of variations, including barrel-aged, habanero, coffee, pumpkin, caramel, vanilla, coconut, and cinnamon roll versions.

Fans just can't get enough Chickow!. Triple Digit launched the League of Extraordinary Chickow!s in 2015: a membership club that allows fans a crack at four exclusive Chickow! beers released in 22-ounce bottles throughout the year, along with glassware, a T-shirt, and growler fills. Two of those were an Irish crème and maple Chickow!

Gilroy enjoys thinking up creative ways to play with the beer.

"It's ever evolving," he says. "It's always that same beer but we hate to see things get stale. Not that that beer really can. But in an environment where there's increasingly more and more awesome beer available at any moment's notice, it's nice to have a beer that constantly challenges you to do something new with it."

Christmas Ale

Great Lakes Brewing Co. | www.greatlakesbrewing.com

Great Lakes Brewing Co.
2516 Market Ave.
Cleveland, Ohio 44113
(216) 771-4404

First brewed: Early 1990s
Style: Winter seasonal
Alcohol content: 7.5 percent
IBUs: 30
Available: For eight weeks starting just before Halloween on draft and in bottles

IF YOU LIKE THIS BEER, here are five other Ohio craft holiday beers to try:

• Thirsty Dog 12 Dogs of Christmas

• Fat Head's Holly Jolly

• MadTree Thunder Snow

• The Brew Kettle Winter Warmer

• Willoughby Wenceslas

Christmas Ale

www.greatlakesbrewing.com | Great Lakes Brewing Co.

REAT LAKES CHRISTMAS ALE isn't just a beer. It's a phenomenon. Despite being distributed only eight weeks of the year, Christmas Ale is the brewery's top-selling brand, thanks to a fanatical following that goes bonkers for the rich combination of honey, cinnamon, and ginger.

Market research firm IRI once pegged it as the most popular craft beer brand in Ohio and one of the top 10 selling brands in the nation during the holiday season—even with its limited release.

The funny thing is that before Great Lakes launched the brand in the early 1990s—the brewery honestly can't remember what year exactly—there really wasn't a Christmas beer style.

Sure, a few breweries put out a holiday brew, such as Sierra Nevada's Celebration Ale. But Great Lakes essentially invented the holiday spiced category. Today, nearly every brewery in northeast Ohio—and many beyond—offers up some variation of Christmas Ale, hoping to piggyback off the public's seemingly insatiable appetite for a seasonal spiced brew.

Each year, Great Lakes hosts a massive release party, complete with a Santa Claus. There's always a line out the door as people scramble to get the first taste of the season.

Hoisting a Christmas Ale has become a holiday tradition, as sacred to some as decorating the Christmas tree or singing carols.

The stories surrounding the beer are legendary. Great Lakes cofounder Pat Conway loves sharing the tale of a traveler who was sitting at the Great Lakes pub at Cleveland Hopkins International Airport sampling the beers. The man loved them. The bartender mentioned that he could buy six-packs to go. The man disappeared, returning later with a suitcase that he stuffed full with Christmas Ale for his journey home.

Clear Sky

Wolf's Ridge Brewing Co. | www.wolfsridgebrewing.com

Wolf's Ridge Brewing Co.
215 N. 4th St.
Columbus, Ohio 43215
(614) 429-3936

First brewed: 2014
Style: Cream ale
Alcohol content: 5 percent
IBUs: 14
Available: Year-round on draft
and in bottles

**IF YOU LIKE THIS BEER, here are
five other Ohio craft beers to try:**

- JAFB Wooster Wayne County
  Cream Ale

- Fifth Street Cure-Ale Cream Ale

- FigLeaf Basmati Cream Ale

- Star City Viking Cream

- Butcher and the Brewer The Jake

Clear Sky

www.wolfsridgebrewing.com | Wolf's Ridge Brewing Co.

ALAN SZUTER wasn't sold on the idea. His first brewer wanted to make a cream ale. But Szuter, who launched the Columbus brewpub and tasting room with his son Bob, wanted his craft brewery to be taken seriously.

His hesitation is understandable. With their light, easy-drinking profiles and use of corn, cream ales don't have the greatest reputation among hardcore craft beer fans, who would prefer to gobble up a hoppy India pale ale or robust Russian imperial stout.

"My initial reaction was: Really? Cream ale?" Szuter recalls. "My correlation and history is Genny Cream, which is not a bad beer, but it's just not a craft beer that comes immediately to mind. But he persisted and brewed it, and it immediately became one of our top sellers. We've kept it on ever since."

Cream ales tend to fill a real need at a craft brewery. Not only are they easy to pound, thanks to the lower alcohol and crisp finish, but they also appeal to that beer drinker who's into Budweiser, Miller, and Coors and is just dipping his or her toe into the craft pool.

Clear Sky, which employs flaked maize, got its name thanks to its clear appearance and the feeling that it's the perfect brew to just kick back with while sitting in a deck chair. It was one of the first beers that Wolf's Ridge packaged for retail sale.

"We try to focus on really drinkable beers," Szuter says. "Even our big ABV beers are really drinkable. You don't taste the alcohol."

Award-winning brewer Chris Davison also has had a lot of fun with Clear Sky, creating plenty of different infused variations. They include the popular Clear Sky Daybreak, which is a coffee-vanilla version, and Clear Sky Cinnamon Toast Brunch, Clear Sky Creamsicle, Clear Sky Lemon Meringue, and Clear Sky Coconut Cream Pie.

Dortmunder Gold Lager

Great Lakes Brewing Co. | www.greatlakesbrewing.com

Great Lakes Brewing Co.
2516 Market Ave.
Cleveland, Ohio 44113
(216) 771-4404

First brewed: 1988
Style: German export bier
Alcohol content: 5.8 percent
IBUs: 30
Awards: Gold medal in 1990 at the Great American Beer Festival
Available: Year-round on draft and in bottles

IF YOU LIKE THIS BEER, here are five other Ohio craft beers to try:

- Thirsty Dog Labrador Lager
- Fat Head's Starlight Lager
- Black Cloister Helles Angel
- Warped Wing Trotwood
- Lager Heads Barnburner Lager

Dortmunder Gold Lager

www.greatlakesbrewing.com | Great Lakes Brewing Co.

D ORTMUNDER GOLD LAGER was one of the first two beers ever made by Great Lakes Brewing. The other was Eliot Ness Amber Lager. But in the beginning, way back in 1988, you couldn't walk into the Great Lakes brewpub and order a Dortmunder. The bartender would give you a quizzical look and wonder if you were in the wrong brewery.

See, Dortmunder wasn't always known as Dortmunder. At the outset, it was called Heisman, named after John Heisman, a famous collegiate football player and coach who grew up in the Ohio City neighborhood that houses the brewery. Heisman was the beer that won a gold medal at the Great American Beer Festival in 1990.

Then the lawyers came calling. Great Lakes received a threatening letter from a high-powered Manhattan law firm representing the Downtown Athletic Club. For nonsports fans, that's the group that hands out the Heisman Trophy each year to the best collegiate football player. The Heisman Trophy is named after, you guessed it, John Heisman. Basically, the letter said, quit using the Heisman name.

The funny thing is cofounder Pat Conway remembers being out in Denver for the beer festival and people mispronouncing the beer's name. They called it Heez-man. Nobody back then associated the beer with football unless you struck the famous Heisman Trophy pose.

Instead of putting up a fight, Great Lakes decided to change the name. But to what? They stumbled over their options until original brewer Thaine Johnson's wife made a simple suggestion: "It's gold in color. Why don't you call it Dortmunder Gold? You just won a gold medal."

The name stuck. Great Lakes helped bring back the Dortmunder style, which is not dry and is more balanced than, as Conway puts it, "tasteless American lagers."

For years, Dortmunder Gold Lager was the best-selling brand for Great Lakes. It has been surpassed only by Christmas Ale.

Great Lakes still pays tribute to the Heisman legacy. As a little joke, the brewery snuck the image of a football onto its label when the labels were redesigned in 2015.

Dreamsicle

MadTree Brewing Co. | www.madtreebrewing.com

MadTree Brewing Co.
3301 Madison Road
Cincinnati, Ohio 45209
(513) 836-8733

First brewed: 2014
Style: Kolsch
Alcohol content: 4.7 percent
IBUs: 11
Available: Year-round on draft

IF YOU LIKE THIS BEER, here are five other Ohio craft beers to try:

- Land-Grant Creamsikolsch
- Taft's Nellie's Key Lime Caribbean Ale
- Christian Moerlein Strawberry Pig
- Mt. Carmel Hibiscus Blueberry Blonde
- Numbers Apple Ale

Dreamsicle

www.madtreebrewing.com | MadTree Brewing Co.

MADTREE COFOUNDER Brady Duncan is the first to admit that Dreamsicle started off as a silly beer.

How else would you describe a brew that mirrors the flavor of a Creamsicle? Remember the orange Popsicle wrapped around ice cream that overwhelms your palate with orange-and-vanilla goodness? Well, that's Dreamsicle.

MadTree created the beer as part of a competition among beer bloggers in 2014. To produce it, MadTree took its kolsch Lift and aged it with orange peel and vanilla beans.

The beer proved so popular that the brewery opted to keep making it. It's now regularly one of the top three drafts sold in the taproom.

"Maybe it started off a bit silly but it's a really good beer," Duncan says. "Those two flavors really play well together."

Dreamsicle has gained a cult following in the Cincinnati area. Because it's available only on draft and has limited distribution outside the brewery taproom, MadTree fans are always clamoring to have the brewery release it in cans.

MadTree played a joke—some may say a cruel joke—on Dreamsicle lovers on April Fool's Day in 2016 saying it would soon package the beer. (Here's a lesson: Don't believe any posts by MadTree on April Fool's, because the brewery has a history of having fun on that day.) As part of the gag, MadTree released an orange Dreamsicle featuring an octopus eating an ice cream cone. Not everyone got the joke.

Later that year, super fan Adam Marcum of Fort Wright, Kentucky, even launched an online petition—all in fun, of course—to urge the brewery to can the beer. Hundreds of people signed it. Duncan says MadTree appreciates the passion.

And while there were no immediate plans to package Dreamsicle, Duncan notes, "There's always a possibility."

Edmund Fitzgerald

Great Lakes Brewing Co. | www.greatlakesbrewing.com

Great Lakes Brewing Co.
2516 Market Ave.
Cleveland, Ohio 44113
(216) 771-4404

First brewed: 1991
Style: American porter
Alcohol content: 5.8 percent
IBUs: 37
Awards: Gold medals in 1991, 1993, and 2002; silver in 2007; and bronze in 2004 at the Great American Beer Festival. Silver medal in 1998 and bronze in 1996 at the World Beer Cup.
Available: Year-round on draft and in bottles

IF YOU LIKE THIS BEER, here are five other Ohio craft beers to try:

- Thirsty Dog Old Leghumper
- Fat Head's Battle Axe Baltic Porter
- Willoughby Gutterpup Porter
- MadTree Identity Crisis
- Fifty West Paycheck's Porter

Edmund Fitzgerald

www.greatlakesbrewing.com | Great Lakes Brewing Co.

W HEN IT comes to award-winning beers produced in Ohio, nothing matches Great Lakes Edmund Fitzgerald Porter—or just Eddie Fitz, if you have a good enough relationship with the brew.

The beer has won seven medals at the Great American Beer Festival and World Beer Cup over the years. No other Ohio-made beer can match that.

It is considered one of the quintessential robust porters in the United States. Need proof? The Beer Judge Certification Program guidelines, which provide a rundown of the ideal aroma, appearance, flavor, and mouthfeel for each style, list Edmund Fitzgerald first among the perfect commercial examples of its style.

Cofounders and brothers Pat and Dan Conway consider that high praise, especially for a beer that's not among Great Lakes' best sellers.

Edmund Fitzgerald came about because the brewpub used to serve Guinness when it first opened. The Conways quickly wondered why they were serving someone else's brand when they could produce their own dark beer, a roasted, chocolaty brew they dubbed Edmund Fitzgerald.

The name pays tribute to a friend's father, 62-year-old John McCarthy, who died aboard the *SS Edmund Fitzgerald* when the freighter sank in Lake Superior in November 1975 during a major storm. All 29 men aboard lost their lives.

McCarthy was the first mate; the voyage was supposed to be his last before he retired. The Conways reached out to the McCarthy family to make sure it was all right to use the Edmund Fitzgerald name.

The beer label features an image of the ship careening through the choppy Lake Superior waters and shares the story of John McCarthy.

Edmund Fitzgerald turned out to be matriarch Margaret Conway's favorite Great Lakes beer.

"She wasn't a beer drinker," Pat Conway recalls. "She liked martinis, but she liked our porter."

Ermal's Belgian Style Cream Ale

Warped Wing Brewing Co. | www.warpedwing.com

Warped Wing Brewing Co.
26 Wyandot St.
Dayton, Ohio 45402
(937) 222-7003

First brewed: 2014
Style: Cream ale
Alcohol content: 5.4 percent
IBUs: 20
Available: Year-round in
16-ounce cans

IF YOU LIKE THIS BEER, here are five other lighter Ohio craft beers to try:

- Sibling Revelry Lavender Wit
- Millersburg Lot 21 Blonde
- Rhinegeist Cougar
- FigLeaf Basmati Cream Ale
- Royal Docks 67 Alaska

Ermal's Belgian Style Cream Ale

www.warpedwing.com | Warped Wing Brewing Co.

ERMAL "ERNIE" FRAZE is one of the most important figures in the history of beer. Don't know him? Well, he invented the pull-top can in 1959: an invention that meant beer drinkers, and soda drinkers for that matter, didn't have to carry around a can opener to enjoy a brew.

Fraze, who founded the Dayton Reliable Tool Company, was at a picnic one day and, alas, had forgotten his can opener. He ended up using a car bumper to open his beer and decided that day that he was going to create a better can. The Ohio Historical Society estimates that more than 75 percent of American breweries were using his invention by 1965.

Warped Wing Ermal's Belgian Style Cream Ale pays tribute to Fraze, not only with the name, but, in a sense, also with the beer itself, which is a style invented by brewmaster John Haggerty.

Cofounders Joe Waizmann, Nick Bowman, and Haggerty knew they wanted to offer an approachable beer in their initial lineup for Warped Wing, which opened in a former industrial building in downtown Dayton in early 2014. Waizmann and Bowman suggested a cream ale, a style with a deep history in southwest Ohio, thanks to Little Kings Cream Ale and a slew of former Dayton breweries that made it.

But, at first, the bearded Haggerty put the kibosh on that idea. He had nothing against cream ales, but the style just didn't speak to him. So he set about to create his own variant. Ermal's Belgian Style Cream Ale is a mash-up of a wit and a cream ale made with corn sugar, coriander, grains of paradise, orange and lemon peel, white pepper, camomile, and flaked oatmeal.

"It all kind of works together flavorwise," Haggerty said.

Ermal's has gone on to become the brewery's best-selling brand. Today, the name Ermal is making a comeback in the Dayton community, and Fraze's story—featured on Ermal's 16-ounce can—is reaching a whole new generation.

"What's impressive and cool for us is that the word 'Ermal' wasn't in our daily lexicon," Waizmann said. "A word like Ermal didn't exist, and now people are relating to the word and associating it with the brewery."

The Evangelist

Staas Brewing Co. | www.staasbrewing.com

Staas Brewing Co.
31 W. Winter St.
Delaware, Ohio 43015
(740) 417-4690

First brewed: 2013
Style: Belgian dark strong ale
Alcohol content: 10 percent
IBUs: 20
Available: Year-round on draft

IF YOU LIKE THIS BEER, here are five other Ohio craft beers to try:

- Maize Valley Monk in Public
- Toxic XXXX
- Fat Head's Sorcerer
- Willoughby Brute's Quad
- Fifty West 4X4 Quadruple

The Evangelist

www.staasbrewing.com | Staas Brewing Co.

MANY BREWERIES love to say that their beers are brewed in small batches. Staas Brewing's The Evangelist, a beautiful Belgian-style quadrupel ale, really is.

Staas, a nanobrewery in Delaware, operates with a half-barrel brewing system. The Evangelist is so big with its grain bill that Staas can produce only 10 gallons at a time on its system. And it's not an easy process, with a two-hour boil required. Despite the challenge, the beer is on draft year-round to the delight of Belgian beer fans.

"It's a labor of love," says Liz Staas, who runs the operation and brews along with her husband, Donald.

The Evangelist was designed by Liz's dad, Tony Evangelista, a homebrewer who started back in the 1970s. He was always a huge fan of Belgian and English beers, and his daughter caught on to Belgians as well, so it should come as no surprise that the brewery specializes in—what else?—Belgian and English styles.

The Evangelist, thanks to its high (10 percent) alcohol by volume, is served in a 10-ounce snifter. It's boozy and dark with plenty of sweetness that gives way to fig, raisin, and plum notes. It was important for Liz Staas to have the fig showcased.

"I really wanted to have a beer that had a lot of fig notes in it because I really like figs, and my dad has a fig tree," Liz Staas says. "That's really where it started. Originally it was supposed to be dubbel, but my dad, in true fashion, was like, 'Let's just blow the grain bill up.' The man doesn't brew session beers. He just doesn't."

Staas worked hard to develop that fig flavor. But Donald Staas isn't willing to disclose how they get it, calling it "top secret."

The beer's name, if you haven't figured it out yet, is a tribute to the Evangelista family.

Fiction

Rhinegeist Brewery | www.rhinegeist.com

Rhinegeist Brewery
1910 Elm St.
Cincinnati, Ohio 45202
(513) 381-1367

First brewed: 2013
Style: Belgian pale ale
Alcohol content: 6 percent
IBUs: 40
Available: May to July on draft and in cans

IF YOU LIKE THIS BEER, here are five other Ohio craft Belgian-style beers to try:

- Staas Golden Delicious
- Rockmill Tripel
- Fat Head's Zeus Juice
- JAFB Wooster Farmyard Pale Ale
- Hoof Hearted Tub Life

Fiction

www.rhinegeist.com | Rhinegeist Brewery

FICTION DOESN'T fit into any particular beer style. Sure, it's a Belgian-style pale ale. There are plenty of those around. But Fiction is light in color, thanks to pilsner malts, designed to resemble sunshine and not the darker hue of traditional Belgian pale ales. Rhinegeist, which produces a slew of pale ales, calls it a Belgian Xtra pale ale because of the color.

Then there's the Rochefort yeast, typically used in darker beers. Fiction also employs Nelson Sauvin hops from New Zealand.

"We thought it would be quirky and weird, and we liked it, but nobody else would understand it," brewery cofounder Bryant Goulding says. "If someone walks up to our table at the Great American Beer Festival and they have time for only one beer, that's the beer I want you to try. I love the fact that it's unlike anything that we've ever had."

The beer is named Fiction because it's a work of fiction, a blend of different ideas. The Cincinnati brewery also has an India pale ale named Truth, and Rhinegeist got a kick out of having beers called Truth and Fiction.

Goulding jokes that the beer was almost called Friction because of the creative tension when the brewery first designed the brew. There was a little struggle over creating a traditional Belgian-style pale ale versus the "rays of sunshine" that Goulding desired.

Not every beer should be brewed to a defined style, Goulding says. "It's really drinkable and really unique. With that Sauvignon Blanc character, I feel like it's going to appeal to wine drinkers. Yet it has enough hop character that us hopheads really enjoy it."

Frog's Hollow Double Pumpkin

Hoppin' Frog Brewery | www.hoppinfrog.com

Hoppin' Frog Brewery
1680 E. Waterloo Road
Akron, Ohio 33406
(330) 352-4578

First brewed: 2009
Style: Autumn seasonal
Alcohol content: 8.4 percent
IBUs: 7.3
Awards: Gold medal at the 2010
Great American Beer Festival
Available: September through
November on draft and in bottles

**IF YOU LIKE THIS BEER, here are
five other Ohio craft beers to try:**

• MadTree The Great Pumpcan

• Thirsty Dog Pumpkin Ale

• BottleHouse Jakt

• Sideswipe Squashing Pumpkins

• Rivertown Pumpkin Ale

Frog's Hollow Double Pumpkin

www.hoppinfrog.com | Hoppin' Frog Brewery

HOPPIN' FROG BREWERY owner and brewer Fred Karm wasn't sure what to name his new pumpkin beer. And then inspiration hit in the form of the Black Sabbath song "Lady Evil."

Karm, a heavy metal fan, heard the first line, "There's a place just south of Witches' Valley," and he started singing along with his own made-up lyrics:

There's a place just south they call Frog's Hollow,
Brewin' pumpkin ale in Fall,
And they only speak in whispers of the name.
There's a lady they say who has the secret,
Of spices picked just right.
With a crying shout, she'll knock it out,
And hand you the Frog's delight.

The beer would be called Frog's Hollow Double Pumpkin Ale, and Karm decided to put his lyrics on the beer label. But at the last minute, he had second thoughts. Then, as if Ronnie James Dio were speaking directly to him while he was brewing the pumpkin beer, the Black Sabbath song came over the radio. That was the sign he needed to stick with his plan.

The beer went on to win a gold medal in 2010 at the Great American Beer Festival. Karm had opted to brew a pumpkin beer because he recalled making one as a homebrewer a decade earlier. A friend had given him a recipe for her pumpkin pie, which featured a combination of eight spices, and they replicated the flavor in a beer.

He made one change from his homebrewer days. He placed real pumpkin in a pizza oven and caramelized some of the fruit. He credits the smoothness of the beer to using Penzeys spices.

"I like pumpkin pie, but I love pumpkin beers," Karm says. "People seem to love it. People are blown away at how much it tastes like a pumpkin pie and how nonoffensive it is. A lot of people are afraid of beers like that."

Ghost Scorpion Lager

Elevator Brewing Co. | www.elevatorbrewery.com

Elevator Brewing Co.
165 N. Fourth St.
Columbus, Ohio 43215
(614) 679-2337

First brewed: 2012
Style: Spiced beer
Alcohol content: 5 percent
IBUs: 13
Available: February in bottles

IF YOU LIKE THIS BEER, here are five other Ohio craft beers to try:

- Rivertown Death
- Toxic Porn or Pawn Pepper
- North High Jalamima
- Phoenix Santa Muerte Spiced Imperial Chocolate Stout
- Columbus Habanero Bodhi

Ghost Scorpion Lager

www.elevatorbrewery.com | Elevator Brewing Co.

ELEVATOR BREWING owner Dick Stevens offers this advice to anyone wanting to sample Ghost Scorpion Lager: Don't drink it. It's not that he wants to discourage people from sampling his beer, he just feels the need to issue a friendly warning. The beer is *freakin' hot*. The brewery makes this claim on the bottle: "The World's Hottest Beer."

Ghost Scorpion is made with both scorpion and ghost chilies, two peppers that far exceed 1 million on the Scoville scale, which measures heat in peppers. Jalapeños are mild in comparison. They clock in anywhere from 2,500 to 8,000 on the scale.

Elevator created the beer with the help of CaJohns Fiery Foods for the Fiery Foods Festival, held each February at the North Market in Columbus. That's where heat seekers gather for, what else, scorching food and drink.

The inaugural batch of Ghost Scorpion Lager is legendary. It initially included six pounds of peppers, but that didn't seem quite enough.

"I tasted it one night and it was knocking me back, hurting me," Stevens says. "But I thought to myself, if I can drink this, it's probably not hot enough."

So the brewery pureed fresh ghost peppers and added them to the beer, making it even hotter. It was served on draft at the Fiery Foods event with pureed peppers floating in the beer. Ghost Scorpion proved too much for some heat seekers who vomited after drinking it. *No foolin'*. The festival organizers asked the brewery to stop serving it.

Elevator, which has backed off the heat just a bit from that first year, has garnered international attention because of the brew. Ghost Scorpion is made only once a year around the time of the Fiery Foods Festival. The brewery has to be extra careful when making it. Workers, who wear gloves, have to bottle it by hand because they don't want the peppers to contaminate the bottling line.

"As long as we don't kill anybody, we should keep doing it and have a little fun along the way," Stevens says.

Head Hunter IPA

Fat Head's Brewery | www.fatheadsbeer.com

Fat Head's Brewery

Production brewery/tasting room:
17450 Engle Lake Drive
Middleburg Heights, Ohio 44130*
(216) 898-0242

Brewpub:
24581 Lorain Road
North Olmsted, Ohio 44070
(440) 801-1001

First brewed: 2009

Style: India pale ale

Alcohol content: 7.5 percent

IBUs: 87

Awards: Silver medals at the 2012 and 2014 World Beer Cup; silver (2010) and bronze (2011) medals at Great American Beer Festival

Available: Year-round on draft and in bottles

IF YOU LIKE THIS BEER, here are five other Ohio craft IPAs to try:

- JAFB Wooster Rain Delay IPA
- Hoof Hearted Musk of the Minotaur
- Platform Speed Merchant
- Willoughby Moondance
- Rhinegeist Truth

*Opening November 2017

Head Hunter IPA

www.fatheadsbeer.com | Fat Head's Brewery

I F THERE were a king of India pale ales in Ohio, Fat Head's Head Hunter would wear the crown. It's hard to argue against this being the top IPA made in the state, given its history of winning awards at major festivals.

Shortly after Fat Head's Brewery and Saloon opened in North Olmsted, co-owner and brewer Matt Cole stuffed his new Head Hunter IPA into a suitcase and shipped it off to The Bistro's IPA Festival in Hayward, California. There, the West Coast–style Head Hunter became the first East Coast India pale ale to take home the gold medal.

That honor in 2009 solidly put the new Fat Head's Brewery on the beer map for IPA drinkers nationwide and helped build the Fat Head's brand. Let's face it, the craft beer world nowadays revolves around IPAs. Since that first win, Head Hunter has gone on to earn another gold medal at The Bistro's fest, a silver and a bronze at the Great American Beer Festival, and two silvers at the World Beer Cup, and twice was crowned the winner of the Brewing News National IPA Championship, proving that it is one of the elite IPAs on the planet.

Ironically, Fat Head's didn't even enter the beer in the 2009 Great American Beer Festival. Cole admits he had no confidence at first about going up against other world-class IPAs.

Fat Head's markets the dry-hopped beer as uncivilized and aggressive—a slogan Cole stole from Wikipedia while researching potential names for the brew. The expression is appropriate, with Head Hunter featuring intense pine, grapefruit, and citrus characteristics.

The amazing thing is that the beer has evolved over the years and will keep evolving year to year, Cole says, based on hop harvests. Citra and Mosaic hops are now part of the recipe. And hop pellets have given way to whole flowers. Despite the yearly changes, Head Hunter keeps winning over the judges and beer fans.

"If you go anywhere in the country right now and mention Fat Head's, they're not going to say Fat Head's makes awesome beer," Cole says. "They're going to say Head Hunter. That's really what we're known for."

Hop JuJu

Fat Head's Brewery | www.fatheadsbeer.com

Fat Head's Brewery

Production brewery/tasting room:
17450 Engle Lake Drive
Middleburg Heights, Ohio 44130*
(216) 898-0242

Brewpub:
24581 Lorain Road
North Olmsted, Ohio 44070
(440) 801-1001

First brewed: 2009
Style: Double India pale ale
Alcohol content: 9 percent
IBUs: 100
Awards: Gold (2013, 2015) and bronze (2016) medals at the Great American Beer Festival; gold medal at the 2016 World Beer Cup
Available: February and March on draft and in bottles

IF YOU LIKE THIS BEER, here are five other Ohio craft beers to try:

- The Brew Kettle El Lupulo Libre
- Columbus Creeper
- Great Lakes Chillwave
- Rhinegeist Saber Tooth Tiger
- MadTree Galaxy High

*Opening November 2017

Hop JuJu

www.fatheadsbeer.com | Fat Head's Brewery

T HE CRITICISM stung and was confusing. Fat Head's co-owner and brewer Matt Cole had sent his new imperial India pale ale called Hop JuJu to the Great American Beer Festival, and one judge was blunt in his assessment. Cole still remembers the feedback: "Reckless use of hops."

He laughs about it now, but there was a time when Cole wasn't very confident in brewing an imperial IPA. That's hard to believe, given the awards that he's won for his hop-forward brews.

Cole, who had already received awards for his Head Hunter IPA, was inspired to make an imperial IPA by breweries such as Russian River, Firestone Walker, and Three Floyds. If they could do it, why couldn't he?

At first, he was making Hop JuJu only once a year. He attributes his shaky confidence to the fact that he wasn't brewing it all the time. Practice does make perfect, so the brewery started making the beer twice and then even four times a year, just to dial in the quality. Then in 2013, after the recipe was tweaked and whole flower hops were added in the finish, the beer took home the gold medal at the Great American Beer Festival.

"To this date, that's my proudest brewing award ever," Cole says. "The IPAs are great. We've done that before. The double was just a 'Wow. Holy shit.' We're really, really onto something."

He also has never forgotten that judge's comment. But Cole got the last laugh.

"We actually use that as a tagline for that beer: Reckless use of hops," he says.

Humulus Nimbus

Seventh Son Brewing Co. | www.seventhsonbrewing.com

Seventh Son Brewing Co.
1101 N. Fourth St.
Columbus, Ohio 43201
(614) 421-2337

First brewed: 2013
Style: India pale ale
Alcohol content: 6 percent
IBUs: 53
Available: Year-round on draft
and in cans

**IF YOU LIKE THIS BEER, here are
five other Ohio craft beers to try:**

• JAFB Wooster Wooster Pale Ale

• Yellow Springs Zoetic

• Rhinegeist Mosaic Pale Ale

• Fat Head's Trail Head Pale Ale

• North High Pale Ale

Humulus Nimbus

www.seventhsonbrewing.com | Seventh Son Brewing Co.

HUMULUS NIMBUS isn't just some ordinary pale ale. It's a super pale ale. It says so right on the blue can. So what is a super pale ale? Well, you can interpret it two different ways. For starters, it's pretty darn tasty. It's also a little stronger than a regular American pale ale, a style that seems to have given way to India pale ales.

Seventh Son is quite proud of the beer, partly because it highlights Mosaic hops. At the time it was first brewed, Mosaic wasn't a common hop, but co-owner Collin Castore and brewer Colin Vent got a tip that it would be the next big thing. They decided to give Mosaic a try and feature it in the third beer they ever produced.

"We put [Mosaic] in there and we really liked it," Vent says. "Shortly thereafter Mosaic started showing up everywhere. All of a sudden, we're like, 'Holy crap, we're sitting on a gold mine.' We had no idea that we had inadvertently contracted for a new really hot hop. That was kind of nice for us to be straight out of the gate with this hop."

They kicked around a few names, including White Rabbit, but settled on Humulus Nimbus. Humulus is another word for hop. Castore also happened to be glancing skyward at the time the name was created; that's the origin of nimbus, a type of cloud.

Humulus Nimbus started out as a summer seasonal. But Seventh Son fans thought otherwise and scarfed down the brew so quickly that it became a year-round beer—one that the Columbus brewery enjoys infusing with habanero, pineapple, chocolate, and vanilla during special cask releases. The super pale ale has turned into the brewery's number-one seller.

"It's a real nice crisp showcase of the hops," Castore says, trying to explain the beer's popularity. "There's hop complexity there. It's not just one-note citrus. It has a crisp body."

Vent designed the beer to have restrained bitterness. "It is bitter, but it's not as bitter as it could be," he says. "I made that decision in the beginning. I do these tours and tell people that I'm never going to brew the most bitter beer that you've ever had. It doesn't interest me. I don't think they're fun to drink. I think everything should be in balance."

Jack Hammer

The Brew Kettle | www.thebrewkettle.com

The Brew Kettle
8377 Pearl Road
Strongsville, Ohio 44136
(440) 239-8788

First brewed: 2008
Style: English barley wine
Alcohol content: 11 percent
IBUs: 40
Awards: Bronze medal at the 2010 Great American Beer Festival. First place at the annual Coles Barley Wine Competition in 2010 and 2012, and second place in 2011
Available: Winter on draft and in bottles

IF YOU LIKE THIS BEER, here are five other Ohio craft beers to try:

- Fifty West 10 & 2 Barley Wine
- Jackie O's Brick Kiln Barley Wine
- Thirsty Dog Bernese Barley Wine Ale
- Seventh Son Ladies and Gentlemen Barley Wine Style Ale
- Barley's Barley Wine

Jack Hammer

www.thebrewkettle.com | The Brew Kettle

JACK KEPHART enjoyed the barley wine at The Brew Kettle when he first arrived as head brewer. But he didn't love it.

The beer, then called Friends of the Brewery Barley Wine, was an American barley wine. In other words, it had a bigger hop note on the aroma and more bitterness in the flavor than he wanted. Kephart much prefers the English barley wines, which are more balanced than their American counterparts.

So he retooled the recipe and rebranded it as Jack Hammer English-Style Barley Wine. Well, he didn't name the beer. His former boss, Chris McKim, thought it would be funny to include Jack's first name in every beer he designed. (There's also One-Eyed Jack Robust Porter. Jack Saison Off didn't make the cut, though.)

Jack Hammer has gone on to become the most awarded beer made by The Brew Kettle. It has won twice and finished second once at the annual Coles Barley Wine Competition, which is sponsored by the *Brewing News*; it also took home a bronze medal at the 2010 Great American Beer Festival.

"It's a sipping beer," says Kephart, who bears a slight resemblance to actor and game show host Drew Carey in his younger days. "You put it in a snifter and sit and relax."

Nellie's Key Lime Caribbean Ale

Taft's Ale House | www.taftsalehouse.com

Taft's Ale House

Brewpub:
1429 Race St.
Cincinnati, Ohio 45202
(513) 334-1393

Production brewery/tasting room:
4831 Spring Grove Ave.
Cincinnati, Ohio 45232

First brewed: 2015
Style: Fruit beer
Alcohol content: 4.7 percent
IBUs: 15
Available: Year-round on draft and in cans

IF YOU LIKE THIS BEER . . . well, Key lime beers are hard to find. But here are five other unusual Ohio craft beers to try:

- Urban Artifact Keypunch Keylime Gose
- Wolf's Ridge Clear Sky Lime Pie
- MadTree Dreamsicle
- Sibling Revelry Lime
- North High Grapefruit Walleye

Nellie's Key Lime Caribbean Ale

www.taftsalehouse.com | Taft's Ale House

T AFT'S ALE HOUSE cofounder and former head brewer Kevin Moreland loves the Florida Keys and has vacationed there ever since he was a kid. He also loves being out on the water and boating. Oh, and he loves Key lime pie, as well.

When he launched Taft's in 2015, he wanted to create a beer that, when he drank it, would whisk his mind to the islands. He's achieved that with Nellie's Key Lime Caribbean Ale, a wheat-based beer with plenty of Key lime aroma and flavor.

"When we're sitting here on a gloomy day, or if you're inside stuck all day, I want people to think they are outside enjoying themselves," Moreland says while sitting in the brewpub as a Bob Marley song plays over the sound system.

He had been making the beer for years as a homebrewer and was just waiting until he owned his own place to roll it out. It's been one of the Cincinnati brewpub's best sellers.

"I'm an unusual brewer," Moreland says. "I don't like to do things by the book."

The name works well on two fronts. The brewpub carries the name of William Howard Taft, the 27th president of the United States and Cincinnati native. Taft's wife, Helen "Nellie" Taft, was known to drink beer and smoke cigarettes.

The beer also features Nellie & Joe's Famous Key West Lime Juice, which gives it that powerful Key lime flavor.

"Those flavors go well in beer for me, especially when it's hot outside," Moreland says. "You want something refreshing. What's more refreshing than a piece of Key lime pie and that beer?"

Nut Brown Ale

Mt. Carmel Brewing Co. | www.mtcarmelbrewingcompany.com

Mt. Carmel Brewing Co.
4362 Mt. Carmel Tobasco Road
Mt. Carmel, Ohio 45244
(513) 240-2739

First brewed: 2008
Style: American brown ale
Alcohol content: 6 percent
IBUs: 38
Awards: Bronze medal at the 2011 International Beer Fest in Cleveland
Available: Year-round in draft and bottles

IF YOU LIKE THIS BEER, here are five other Ohio craft beers to try:

- HiHO TouchDown Brown
- Market Garden Forest City Brown Ale
- Phoenix Danger City Brown Ale
- Eudora Mother-Fuggle Brown Ale
- Yellow Springs Handsome

Nut Brown Ale

www.mtcarmelbrewingcompany.com | Mt. Carmel Brewing Co.

NUT BROWN ALE was the first Mt. Carmel Brewing Co. beer not made in the basement. Seriously. Cofounders Mike and Kathleen Dewey launched their brewery in 2005 in the basement of their Mount Carmel farmhouse—the same one that appears on the beer labels.

A few years into the venture, sales were going well for their original Mt. Carmel Blonde, Amber, and Stout beers. So well, in fact, that the Deweys decided to expand, moving out of the basement and upgrading their brewing system in a new building attached to the back of the house.

They wanted to add a fourth beer so they could start offering a variety pack. Mike opted for a nut brown ale, which became the first new beer recipe made on the new system. He didn't even bother doing a test batch.

"It was literally a one-time trial and error where we did our homework, made the beer, loved it, and never changed it since," Mike Dewey says.

Picking a name was easy. Mt. Carmel doesn't come up with fanciful names for its beers. It sticks with the style. So Nut Brown Ale was a natural.

"I thought it would be cool to brew a beer that just screams its name," Mike Dewey says. "And that's the balance I think we came to find with this beer. You can almost close your eyes and drink it and know what it is every time."

Brown ales, and nut brown ales in particular, aren't the most popular beer styles, so it may be a bit of a surprise that he chose that style as one of the brewery's core brands. But Mike Dewey had always been a big fan of Newcastle Brown Ale. In college, he and his friends would even drive to Dayton to buy kegs because the beer wasn't available in Cincinnati at the time. He also has a pretty simple philosophy when making beer: "I don't brew a beer I don't like."

Nutcase Peanut Butter Porter

Listermann Brewing Co. | www.listermannbrewing.com

Listermann Brewing Co.
1621 Dana Ave.
Cincinnati, Ohio 45207
(513) 731-1130

First brewed: 2012
Style: Specialty
Alcohol content: 6.7 percent
IBUs: 28
Awards: Bronze medal at the 2014
Great American Beer Festival
Available: Year-round on draft
and in bottles

**IF YOU LIKE THIS BEER, here are
five other Ohio craft beers to try:**

• Willoughby Nut Smasher

• Willoughby Peanut Butter
  Coffee Porter

• North River Border Battle Porter

• Hoppin' Frog Infusion A
  Coffee Porter

• Millersburg Nuthouse Peanut
  Butter Porter

Nutcase Peanut Butter Porter

www.listermannbrewing.com | Listermann Brewing Co.

L ISTERMANN BREWING owner Dan Listermann didn't know his
brewers had decided to make a special peanut butter beer for an "End
of the World Party." Remember when the world was supposed to end in
2012, thanks to that supposed hiccup in the Mayan calendar?

The brewery wanted to celebrate. Kevin Moreland, who was the head
brewer at the time, made Nutcase Peanut Butter Porter behind his boss's back,
knowing that Dan Listermann would never approve.

"I didn't find out about it until it was on tap, and I was angry," Dan
Listermann says. "It was the dumbest thing I had ever heard of in my life.
They knew I wouldn't let them do that. I'm glad to be wrong sometimes."

So, so wrong. It's funny how things work out. Nutcase was meant to be a
one-time brew and disappear. But beer drinkers loved it and kept demanding
it. The brewery bowed to its fans and decided to make it again—and again,
and again.

Nutcase not only has gone on to become Listermann's only year-round
brand—in other words, mega-popular for the small Cincinnati brewery—but it
also earned a bronze medal at the 2014 Great American Beer Festival.

The beer's popularity shouldn't be so surprising. Nutcase is different; it
screams peanut butter in the aroma and flavor.

Listermann loves to experiment with beer, even with its established
brews, and Nutcase is no exception. Former head brewer Patrick Gilroy
created a barrel-aged version and—come on now, you were expecting this—
a peanut-butter-and-jelly version. He's also made Nutcase with blackberries
and raspberries.

"Nutcase has been a blast to make," Gilroy says. "All the beers are."

Oil of Aphrodite

Jackie O's Brewery | www.jackieos.com

Jackie O's Brewery

Production brewery/tasting room:
25 Campbell St.
Athens, Ohio 45701
(740) 447-9063

Brewpub:
24 W. Union St.
Athens, Ohio 45701
(740) 592-9686

First brewed: 2010
Style: Imperial stout
Alcohol content: 10 percent
IBUs: 65
Available: Year-round on draft
and in bottles

**IF YOU LIKE THIS BEER, here are
five other Ohio craft beers to try:**

- Hoppin' Frog Cleveland Crusher
- Hoppin' Frog D.O.R.I.S. the
  Destroyer
- Jackie O's Dark Apparition
- MadTree Axis Mundi
- Wolf's Ridge Dire Wolf

Oil of Aphrodite

www.jackieos.com | Jackie O's Brewery

BREWMASTER BRAD CLARK was getting the itch to experiment. He had created a Russian imperial stout called Dark Apparition in 2007. He had fun brewing it, then more fun putting it in bourbon and brandy barrels. And then, a few years later, he got the urge to design another big stout.

A big Frank Zappa fan, Clark pulled inspiration from the song "Cosmik Debris," which includes the goofy line, "with the oil of Aphrodite, and the dust of the grand wazoo." "I loved that lyric, and I thought it lent itself toward a stout," Clark says. "I had it in the back of my head as this experimental second imperial stout."

He just needed to craft the recipe to fit the song. Right then, local farmer Chris Chmiel of Integration Acres, which supplies fresh pawpaws to Jackie O's, mentioned that he had plenty of black walnuts available if Clark wanted to play with those. Just like in the cartoons, a light bulb came on over his head.

He would brew an imperial stout with black walnuts and call it Oil of Aphrodite. Everyone was brewing stouts with coffee and chocolate, but walnuts? Nobody was using walnuts.

Clark roasted the walnuts to pull the oils out of them. He found that the roasting changed the character of the nuts, giving them a blueberry-like fruitiness and adding a level of sweetness. He also used dark Belgian candy syrup to separate the brew's flavor from Dark Apparition.

Oil of Aphrodite—available on draft and in 375-ml bottles—is one of Jackie O's highest rated beers on both BeerAdvocate.com and RateBeer.com.

It's appropriate that the beer has the word oil in its name. Oil of Aphrodite is thick and black as night. And, just as he had done with Dark Apparition, Clark played around with Oil of Aphrodite, aging it in rum barrels.

"That's when things really got hot for us," Clark says. "People started trading for our beers. . . . It was kind of a feverish point at the brewpub. That's really what kind of kicked it off. We were doing a lot of different things before that, but that was the beer that grabbed people's attention."

Ojos Negros

Rivertown Brewing Co. | www.rivertownbrewery.com

Rivertown Brewing Co.

Lockport Barrel House:
607 Shepherd Drive
Lockland, Ohio 45215
(513) 827-9280

Monroe Barrel House:
6550 Hamilton Lebanon Road
Middletown, Ohio 45044
(513) 402-7135

First brewed: 2011
Style: American wild ale
Alcohol content: 6.3 percent
IBUs: 6
Available: Summer on draft
and in bottles

**IF YOU LIKE THIS BEER, here are
five other Ohio craft beers to try:**

• Streetside Raspberry Beret

• Rivertown Old Sour Cherry Porter

• Little Fish Woodthrush

• Jackie O's Funky South Paw

• Urban Artifact The Gadget Sour
  Berry Bomb

Ojos Negros

www.rivertownbrewery.com | Rivertown Brewing Co.

FIRST OFF, Ojos Negros is pronounced Oh-os nay-gros. Not Oh-joes nay-gros. Or Oh-chos nay-gros. But frankly, Rivertown Brewing owner and brewer Jason Roeper doesn't care how you pronounce it, as long as you're ordering it.

Ojos Negros is one of the brewery's seasonal sour beers; the others are Lambic, Old Sour Cherry Porter, Triumvirate, and Ville De Rivere Geuze. But Ojos Negros is perhaps the most well known of the sours, thanks to Charlie Papazian, founder of the Brewers Association and Great American Beer Festival. He raved about the brew in a 2014 review in *All about Beer Magazine*, telling readers if they enjoy sours to seek out the brew.

Made with fresh blackberries and naturally fermented, Ojos Negros is a limited release available only during the summertime. How fresh are those blackberries?

Roeper recalls a man, rage in his face and voice, coming to the brewery to complain that there was a blackberry seed in his beer. Roeper responded, "You're welcome." Then he proceeded to explain how the brewery uses fresh blackberries and not syrup, and how he doesn't filter the brew. He took the man on a tour of the brewery and showed him how they use open fermentation with their sours. The man left happy and a little wiser.

"We produce sours the correct way," Roeper says, trying to explain its popularity. "The most common misconception I see from any beer drinker is that lambics are supposed to be heavily carbonated. The traditionalists, the guys who drink these beers all the time, compliment us. This is the way it's supposed to be. I think that's what sets us apart."

Rivertown has focused more on sour beers since Roeper took sole control of the brewery in 2014. He wants sours to be the brewery's calling card.

"We're not riding the IPA wave," he says. "We're creating a wave."

Oyster Stout

North High Brewing Co. | www.northhighbrewing.com

North High Brewing Co.
1228 N. High St.
Columbus, Ohio 43201
(614) 407-5278

First brewed: 2013
Style: Stout
Alcohol content: 5.5 percent
IBUs: 22
Available: Only on draft at
The Pearl restaurant,
641 N. High St., Columbus, Ohio

**IF YOU LIKE THIS BEER, here are
five other Ohio craft stouts to try:**

- Great Lakes Shuck It Oyster Stout
- Seventh Son Black Sheep
- Millersburg State 39 Stout
- Fifth Street RyRish Dry Irish Stout
- Zaftig Black Perle Stout

Oyster Stout

www.northhighbrewing.com | North High Brewing Co.

ORTH HIGH BREWING co-owners Gavin Meyer and Tim Ward walked into The Pearl one day and noticed that the beer list was missing something. In a restaurant and tavern serving fresh Chesapeake oysters, why wasn't an oyster stout on the menu? Then they realized that their brewery could make one.

The Pearl, a gastropub on Columbus's busy North High Street, took them up on their offer. North High makes a special oyster stout exclusively for The Pearl. It's not even served at the North High taproom just up the street.

And yes, the stout features real Chesapeake oysters, the same kind served raw or cooked at The Pearl.

North High starts with a rich milk stout, then adds 60 oysters to the kettle during the boil, keeping the oysters in a strainer so they don't float away and permeate the brewing equipment. Well, there was that one time they found a tiny crab in the heat exchanger.

The oysters open while cooking in the kettle, releasing their briny goodness and ocean flavor.

"I get a hint of saltiness," brewer Jason McKibben says, explaining the flavor. "That brine really comes through. In the aroma, you get a little bit of the ocean. I don't know what else to call it, but it kind of smells like the ocean. It's a distinctive aroma. But it's subtle. It doesn't overpower the beer."

And what happens to those oysters cooked in the kettle?

"If people are hungry enough, they get eaten," Ward says. "Otherwise, they just get chucked . . . I think once we went through all 60. We had some friends here, and we had a feast."

Panther Hollow

Millersburg Brewing Co. | www.millersburgbrewing.com

Millersburg Brewing Co.
60 E. Jackson St.
Millersburg, Ohio 44654
(330) 674-4728

First brewed: 2013
Style: American porter
Alcohol content: 6.25 percent
IBUs: 38
Available: Year-round
on draft and cans

**IF YOU LIKE THIS BEER, here are
five other Ohio craft beers to try:**

- Rivertown Roebling
- Buckeye Lake Vanilla Porter
- Four String Vanilla Porter
- Hairless Hare CRV Porter
- Star City Vanilla Porter

Panther Hollow

www.millersburgbrewing.com | Millersburg Brewing Co.

MILLERSBURG HEAD BREWER Marty Lindon has a simple explanation for why his Panther Hollow Vanilla Porter is so popular.

"Vanilla just seems to be a big attraction," he says, while sampling the beer in the Millersburg tasting room.

Yes, for many people vanilla is tasty, whether it's in ice cream or a cake or, even, a beer. The only mystery for Lindon is why Panther Hollow is such a big seller on Sundays.

The top-selling beers for Millersburg, a production brewery and tasting room located in the heart of Amish country, are Lot 21 Blonde, French Ridge IPA, and Panther Hollow. But on Sundays, the vanilla porter outsells everything else. Lindon figures that the community gets plenty of tourists on the weekends and a vanilla porter is unusual enough to attract attention.

Millersburg uses both vanilla beans and vanilla extract in the beer, but the vanilla flavor isn't overpowering. That's by design.

"A lot of vanilla porters and vanilla stouts are just over the top," Lindon says. "Panther Hollow has coffee flavors from the coffee malt and chocolate flavors from the chocolate malt that come through along with the vanilla."

The recipe dates back to Lindon's homebrewing days when he made a vanilla bean oatmeal stout. People even joked about farting vanilla the next day. Instead of doing a heavier stout, he opted for a porter. When the brewery first opened, Lindon had two porters available: a robust one and the vanilla version. Everyone quickly gravitated to Panther Hollow, so it became a year-round brew.

The beer is named after Panther's Hollow, an area of Holmes County that's rumored to be haunted.

PawPaw Wheat

Buckeye Brewing Co. | www.buckeyebrewing.com

Buckeye Brewing Co.
9985 Walford Ave.
Cleveland, Ohio 44102
(216) 281-5347

First brewed: 2011
Style: Fruit beer
Alcohol content: 6 to 6.5 percent
IBUs: 15
Available: June through September
on draft and in bottles

**IF YOU LIKE THIS BEER, here are
five other Ohio craft pawpaw
beers to try:**

- Devil's Kettle Devil's Paw
- Jackie O's Paw Paw Wheat
- Marietta Putnam's Pawpaw Ale
- Thirsty Dog Pawpaw Saison
- Weasel Boy Weasel Paw Pawpaw
  Pale Ale

PawPaw Wheat

www.buckeyebrewing.com | Buckeye Brewing Co.

BUCKEYE BREWING owner and brewer Garin Wright started hearing about this native Ohio fruit called the pawpaw when he took part in the first Ohio Brew Week in Athens in 2006. He had no clue what a pawpaw was. But he soon discovered that the fruit—it grows on trees and has a delicate mango-banana-pineapple flavor—is a big deal in southeast Ohio.

"This fruit is given a lot of love in the Hocking Hills," Wright says.

There's even a whole multiday celebration dedicated to it: the annual Ohio Pawpaw Festival, which takes place each September at Lake Snowden in Albany. That's how Wright got involved in making a pawpaw beer. Festival organizer Chris Chmiel, who runs Integration Acres, asked him in 2010 to create a special brew using pawpaws for the next year's event. He's been making one ever since.

Wright turned to the one brewer who, at the time, was making a pawpaw beer. Kelly Sauber, then the head brewer at Marietta Brewing, offered guidance and even shared his recipe with Wright.

Knowing that the pawpaw is a fragile and subtle fruit when it comes to aroma and flavor, Wright designed a wheat beer that wouldn't overwhelm the pawpaw.

Each year, he receives buckets of frozen pawpaw pulp from Chmiel's farm. He takes his wheat beer and lets it sit with the pulp, allowing it to go through a second fermentation. The aroma and flavor of the beer can change from year to year, depending on that year's batch of harvested pawpaw. Wright has been content to release the beer only during the summer because it's particularly tasty on a hot day.

"It's fruity. It's dry. It's not strong. It makes sense that it would work," he says.

And, in general, beer drinkers gobble it up. The only reason he finds that some people don't want to try it is because they are scared and don't know what a pawpaw is.

"They've never heard of it. That's all," Wright says. He's doing his best to change that.

Peanut Butter Cup Coffee Porter

Willoughby Brewing Co. | www.willoughbybrewing.com

Willoughby Brewing Co.
4057 Erie St.
Willoughby, Ohio 44094
(440) 975-0202

First brewed: 2007 or 2008
Style: Specialty
Alcohol content: 5.5 percent
IBUs: 26
Awards: Gold medal at the World Beer Cup in 2014
Available: Year-round on draft

IF YOU LIKE THIS BEER, here are five other Ohio craft beers to try:

- Willoughby Nut Smasher
- Listermann Nutcase Peanut Butter Porter
- Millersburg Nuthouse Peanut Butter Porter
- Hoppin' Frog Infusion A Coffee Porter
- Zaftig Nuttin' 2it

Peanut Butter Cup Coffee Porter

www.willoughbybrewing.com | Willoughby Brewing Co.

FOR YEARS, Willoughby Brewing won praise for its Peanut Butter Cup Coffee Porter, a robust porter infused with locally roasted coffee, peanut butter, and chocolate.

It was always a major hit at festivals, with beer drinkers racing to the Willoughby booth to sample one of the most unusual beers around. It even garnered national attention, ending up on *Bon Appétit* magazine's list of the "Weirdest Beers in America" in 2012.

While head brewer Rick Seibt welcomed the recognition, he bristled at the notion that Peanut Butter Cup Coffee Porter was some sort of oddity—a freak beer to be tasted only because it was weird. Instead, he saw it as an excellent brew that didn't deserve to be pigeonholed into some category reserved for strange concoctions.

Peanut Butter Cup Coffee Porter finally got its just desserts at the 2014 World Beer Cup, taking home a gold medal in the specialty beer category. In that single moment, the beer made a much-deserved leap from weird to award winning. It also cemented Willoughby's reputation nationwide as a solid brewpub.

Since then, *Men's Journal* dubbed Peanut Butter Cup Coffee Porter as one of the "100 Best Beers in the World," turning on a whole new batch of beer drinkers to the brew. The beer had always enjoyed a loyal and fanatical following but the medal and magazine exposure ramped up interest even more.

Because the beer is available only at the brewpub, there are some legendary stories about the lengths people go to get their hands on it. One Saturday, a fella stopped by and bought 30 Crowler cans—$270 worth.

Then there's the story about the guy from Reading, Pennsylvania, who hopped aboard a friend's small Cessna airplane and flew the nearly 400 miles into the nearby Lost Nation Airport just to grab a few growlers to take to a wedding reception.

"It's a unique flavor sensation that I would never try to change or alter at any point of time. Ever," Seibt says. "It's perfect the way it is right now."

Pickle Gose

Urban Artifact | www.artifactbeer.com

Urban Artifact
1662 Blue Rock St.
Cincinnati, Ohio 45223
(513) 620-4729

First brewed: 2015
Style: Gose
Alcohol content: 4.3 percent
IBUs: 12
Available: Limited release on draft and in cans, always available in July during Cincinnati Burger Week

IF YOU LIKE THIS BEER, here are five other Ohio craft beers to try:

- Sibling Revelry Lavender Wit
- Urban Artifact Pinwheel
- MadTree Kum with Me
- Marietta Estella's Raspberry Wheat
- JAFB Wooster Apricot Actually Ale

Pickle Gose

www.artifactbeer.com | Urban Artifact

BREWERS SOMETIMES throw caution to the wind and make something so out there, so creative that even they aren't sure what beer drinkers will think. That's certainly the case with Urban Artifact Pickle Gose.

The Cincinnati brewery specializes in tart and wild beers. Pickle Gose, which made its debut at the brewery's 12 Holiday Beers event in 2015, is right on the mark when it comes to wild—as in wild and crazy.

"It was kind of a shot in the dark, so to speak," cofounder Scotty Hunter says about the original premise. "When you make something divisive in a beer style, it can be a hit or a miss. And it was a hit. It fits who we are as a brand and what we do."

The beer is made with dill grown by Ohio Valley Hops and fresh cucumbers.

"It really tastes like you're biting into a dill pickle," Hunter says. "A lot of people think it will be vinegary. It's more that cucumber and dill flavor, and that bright clean acidity that you get with the pickle and not the juice you get in the jar."

OH! Chips, a boutique chipmaker in Columbus, even created Urban Artifact Spicy Pickle Potato Chips in 2016 to pair with the unusual brew.

Pickle Gose isn't a year-round brew. It's available on a limited basis but it does show up during Cincinnati Burger Week in July. After all, what goes better with a burger than a pickle?

Progress Pilsner

Market Garden Brewery | www.marketgardenbrewery.com

Market Garden Brewery
1947 W. 25th St.
Cleveland, Ohio 44113
(216) 621-4000

First brewed: 2011
Style: Pilsner
Alcohol content: 5.5 percent
IBUs: 45
Awards: Bronze medal at the 2013 Great American Beer Festival
Available: Year-round on draft and in bottles

IF YOU LIKE THIS BEER, here are five other Ohio craft beers to try:

• Goldhorn Polka City Pilsner

• Warped Wing Brasspunk Pils

• Great Lakes Turntable Pils

• Rhinegeist Puma

• Woodburn Steinpils

Progress Pilsner

www.marketgardenbrewery.com | Market Garden Brewery

PERHAPS YOU didn't know this. Heck, it's likely you don't know this unless you're into vexillology, but the official flag for the city of Cleveland features the words "Progress & Prosperity."

The folks behind Market Garden Brewery—who are big boosters of the community and their Ohio City neighborhood in particular—were inspired by that slogan and figured that it would make a perfect name for a beer. That's how Progress Pilsner was born.

"It seems appropriate," brewmaster Andy Tveekrem says. "Our breweries are always a work in progress. Beer is always a work in progress. There's no such thing as a static recipe. We always tweak it a little bit here and there."

Progress Pilsner is a pretty simple beer, featuring a dry, crisp finish. Unfiltered, it was made originally with Saaz hops and German pilsner malt. That's what brought home a bronze medal at the 2013 Great American Beer Festival and cemented the beer's reputation as an easy-drinking beauty.

But, as the name implies, and, as Tveekrem points out, progress was made. The brewery later switched to German Hallertau hops.

Before Market Garden opened its own production brewery, affectionately dubbed the Palace of Fermentation, it was tough to keep the beer on draft at the brewpub, an uptempo, urban spot where a younger crowd often wants to have more than one beer in a sitting.

But it wasn't just that. The beer also is aged for about eight weeks, meaning, as Tveekrem described it, Progress Pilsner is a bit of a tank hog.

Tank hog or not, pilsner is one of Tveekrem's favorite styles.

"These are the kinds of beers that I like to have," he says. "I like pale ales and IPAs, and that's what I usually take home. But, if I'm out and about, I want to have a few and still be able to function."

PsycHOPathy IPA

MadTree Brewing Co. | www.madtreebrewing.com

MadTree Brewing Co.
3301 Madison Road
Cincinnati, Ohio 45209
(513) 836-8733

First brewed: 2013
Style: India pale ale
Alcohol content: 6.9 percent
IBUs: 70
Available: Year-round on draft
and in cans

**IF YOU LIKE THIS BEER, here are
five other Ohio craft beers to try:**

- Phoenix Redemption IPA
- Warped Wing Gamma Bomb
- JAFB Rain Delay IPA
- Jackie O's Mystic Mama
- Brick and Barrel Bitter Chief

PsycHOPathy IPA

www.madtreebrewing.com | MadTree Brewing Co.

EVERY SO OFTEN, a beer comes along that makes a significant mark in brewing history. The first canned beer in the United States was Krueger in 1935. Light beer started with the creation of Meister Brau Lite in 1967. And Albion Ale is credited with being the first microbrew in 1977.

MadTree Brewing Co. made its own history on March 28, 2013. That was the day the first can of MadTree PsycHOPathy rolled off the canning line at the Cincinnati brewery. Cofounders Brady Duncan, Jeff Hunt, and Kenny McNutt chugged the first few cans—apparently a tradition, if you want your brewery to have good luck in the future.

Now, craft beer had been available in cans for years out West and along the East Coast, and several Ohio breweries had talked about canning. But it wasn't until MadTree came along that an Ohio brewery started offering its beer in cans.

Duncan, Hunt, and McNutt chose canning for several reasons, including the fact that cans seal out light and oxygen better than bottles, are less expensive to transport, and are more portable for beer drinkers. Then there's the fact that, as McNutt puts it, "they look really sexy on a retail shelf." Still, there remained a stigma about cans from consumers.

"It really doesn't happen very often now, but when we were in the fundraising stages and even shortly after we started canning, there were still a lot of naysayers about craft beer in a can," McNutt says. "I heard things like 'Good beer comes in a bottle' and 'I love your plan, but cans? Really?' I think the craft beer industry has shown that good beer can definitely come in cans."

PsycHOPathy has been well received by beer drinkers, making up about 30 percent of MadTree sales. The brewery also has picked up positive national publicity thanks to the brew. *Outside* magazine named it one of the best canned beers of 2013. The website Thrillist.com called it one of the coolest beer cans on the market in 2014. And the website Craftcans.com highlighted PsycHOPathy as one of "Six New Craft Can Designs That Belong in an Art Gallery" in 2013.

"I think this is pretty cool," McNutt says about the brewery's place in history.

Rockmill Saison

Rockmill Brewery | www.rockmillbrewery.com

Rockmill Brewery
5705 Lithopolis Road NW
Lancaster, Ohio 43130
(740) 205-8076

Rockmill Tavern
503 S. Front St.
Columbus, Ohio 43215
(614) 732-4364

First brewed: 2010
Style: Saison
Alcohol content: 7 percent
IBUs: 34
Available: Year-round on draft
and in bottles

**IF YOU LIKE THIS BEER, here are
five other Ohio craft beers to try:**

- Sideswipe Coop Looter
- Little Fish Sunfish
- Staas Wildcat Sally
- Fifty West Are We There Yet Saison
- JAFB Wooster Harvest Saison

Rockmill Saison

www.rockmillbrewery.com | Rockmill Brewery

MATTHEW BARBEE will never forget his first saison. He was working as a talent manager in Los Angeles and ordered a Saison Dupont at a restaurant. At the time, he was not a beer fan and was much more passionate about wine.

But he instantly became enamored with Belgian beers, bottle-conditioned brews, and Belgian yeast. When he opened Rockmill Brewery at the family's former horse farm in Lancaster years later, there was no question that he would produce Belgian-style beers or that the first would be a saison, also known as a farmhouse ale.

He called it Saison after the style, which carries a fruity tartness and yeast character in the aroma and flavor. Barbee attributes the simplicity of that name and those of his other brands to his love of wine and how wines are named after their grape varietals.

Saison has become Rockmill's flagship brand. Barbee attributes its popularity in part to the fact that farmhouse ales complement food so well. Famous chef Jonathon Sawyer featured Saison during a James Beard House dinner in 2011—an experience that Barbee considered an honor.

"It was, is, and always will be my beer style," Barbee says. "That's the world that I'm excited to live in and grow in. I'm very excited about craft beer in general, but saison is always going to be where my passion lies. . . . I'll always be excited about doing other beer styles and trying them out, but saisons are always going to be closest to my heart."

Why? It's undeniable that there's a romantic element to the style because it pulled him into craft beer. But he also loves playing with the yeast strain and designing different saisons.

In addition to Saison, the brewery also offers Petit Saison, a lower-alcohol version, and Saison Noire, which features roasted barley.

"I have done a number of variations on our Saison and always will," Barbee says. "I'll probably do a thousand different saisons by the time we're done."

Shroominous

Blank Slate Brewing Co. | www.blankslatebeer.com

Blank Slate Brewing Co.
4233 Airport Road
Cincinnati, Ohio 45226
(513) 979-4540

First brewed: 2012
Style: Brown ale
Alcohol content: 8 percent
IBUs: 40 to 50
Available: Year-round on draft

IF YOU LIKE THIS BEER . . . well, there aren't other mushroom beers around. Here are five other Ohio craft brown ales to try:

- Phoenix Danger City Brown Ale
- Old Firehouse Nutty Pyro
- Land-Grant Son of a Mudder
- MadCap Bad Leroy Brown Ale
- Great Lakes Cleveland Brown Ale

Shroominous

www.blankslatebeer.com | Blank Slate Brewing Co.

INSPIRATION CAN hit anywhere. Blank Slate brewer and owner Scott LaFollette was rehydrating some dried shitake mushrooms for a Chinese stir-fry at home when he got a whiff of the leftover mushroom broth. He tasted it and fell in love with the earthy, woody character.

"I bet this would be a nice savory quality to add to a beer," he thought at the time.

LaFollette, who enjoys designing beers that are a bit off style (see his The Lesser Path, an India white ale), started experimenting with different beer styles, blending in some of the broth. The mushroom flavor disappeared in darker beers, such as porters and stouts, but it came through subtly and played well with a brown ale because of the beer's malty base.

Shroominous was born. To extract the mushroom broth, LaFollette steeps dried shitake mushrooms in a giant tea bag in the wort. And, for the record, while he experimented with different beer styles, he never deviated from shitake mushrooms, his favorite.

The beer can be a tough sell with some people, especially those who don't like mushrooms. That's when LaFollette educates them about the process and stresses that he's created a brown ale with the slight flavor of mushrooms, as opposed to a mushroom-tasting beer.

"Bear in mind, it doesn't taste like eating a handful of mushrooms," he says. "If we didn't say it had mushrooms in it, half the people who try it probably would never pick up that it had mushrooms in it."

He encourages beer drinkers to drink it from a snifter and pair it with food, particularly any grilled meat. He also encourages people to step outside their comfort zone and the familiar when it comes to tasting beer.

"It's always a good idea to give something new a try because you never know until you try it," LaFollette says.

Smokin' Handsome

Yellow Springs Brewery | www.yellowspringsbrewery.com

Yellow Springs Brewery
305 Walnut St.
Yellow Springs, Ohio 45387
(937) 767-0222

First brewed: 2013
Style: Rauchbier
Alcohol content: 5.5 percent
IBUs: 30
Awards: Silver medal at the 2013 Great American Beer Festival
Available: October through December on draft

IF YOU LIKE THIS BEER, here are five other Ohio craft beers to try:

- Sideswipe Elegant Hoodlum
- Thirsty Dog Rail Dog
- Blank Slate Fume
- Lager Heads Smokie Robbins
- Fat Head's Up in Smoke

Smokin' Handsome

www.yellowspringsbrewery.com | Yellow Springs Brewery

YELLOW SPRINGS BREWERY owner Nate Cornett admits that smoke beer isn't exactly the most popular style around. Craft beer drinkers either love the aroma and flavor imparted by the smoked malts, or they despise those characteristics, feeling like they are licking an ashtray.

"We're big fans of all styles," Cornett says. "Smoke beers are something that a lot of people don't do. We try to set ourselves apart, and that was important to us, especially early on, trying to do beers that other breweries weren't doing locally."

Brewer Jeffrey McElfresh happens to be one of those who adore the style. So he designed a brown ale with 20 percent smoked malts. The beer, called Smokin' Handsome, has brought plenty of recognition to the small brewery in Yellow Springs thanks to its winning a silver medal at the 2013 Great American Beer Festival.

Yellow Springs had just opened, and Cornett wanted to submit beers to the prestigious competition. But when the brewery tried to enter, it was shut out of its preferred categories. In fact, Smokin' Handsome was the only beer it ended up entering. It made for a great story: New brewery enters one beer and wins.

"I describe it as rich, chocolaty, roasty, with a little bit of campfire," Cornett says. "It's a German beechwood smoke flavor, so it lends itself almost more to bacon than campfire."

Despite the smoke character, some people confuse Smokin' Handsome with another beer on the menu. Yellow Springs also makes Handsome, the same brown ale without the smoked malts. Smokin' Handsome is available only from October to December; however, some customers, during other months, think they are drinking the smoke beer when they actually are drinking the regular brown ale.

Cornett finds it funny when people praise the wrong beer. He always laughs and takes the compliment in stride, responding, "We haven't made Smokin' Handsome for six months, but thank you."

Summer Teeth

Columbus Brewing Co. | www.columbusbrewing.com

Columbus Brewing Co.
2555 Harrison Road
Columbus, Ohio 43204
(614) 224-3626

First brewed: 2008
Style: German-style lager
Alcohol content: 5 percent
IBUs: Low 20s
Awards: Bronze medal at the 2010
Great American Beer Festival
Available: May and June on draft
and in bottles

**IF YOU LIKE THIS BEER, here are
five other easy-drinking Ohio craft
beers to try:**

• Buckeye Martian Marzen Lager

• Jackie O's Ricky

• Fat Head's Starlight Lager

• Double Wing POC

• Market Garden Progress Pilsner

Summer Teeth

www.columbusbrewing.com | Columbus Brewing Co.

REMEMBER THAT song "One of These Things (Is Not Like the Others)" from the famous children's television program *Sesame Street*? Basically, the characters would look at several items and try to pick out the one that didn't belong. A saw, a screwdriver, a hammer, and a shoe? The shoe, obviously.

Well, that song could be playing in the background at Columbus Brewing. The brewery has built its reputation on beautiful, high-hopped brews like Bodhi, Creeper, and Uncle Rusty. Then all of a sudden, there's Summer Teeth, an unfiltered kellerbier.

It's super-easy to drink and it's the lightest beer in the Columbus portfolio. Owner and brewer Eric Bean, who's a big fan of German-style beers, wanted to make a great summer brew.

"Summer seasonals are the most boring seasonals," he says. "But they are so good. We wanted to design a beer that you could pound. I don't know if that's the right way of saying it. Something you could drink and consume on a hot day. That's a better way of saying it."

Summer Teeth also was the first beer in the Columbus lineup with a fanciful name. Early names just reflected the style such as IPA, Pale Ale, Saison, and Belgian Dark Strong Ale. Obviously, many imaginative brand names have followed.

Bean says he can't remember how Summer Teeth got its name. There's *Summerteeth*, the third album by alternative rock band Wilco. So it could be that. And then Bean, who likes to leave people guessing when it comes to his beer brands, shares another theory related to a quote about Appalachian female hillbillies and their dental hygiene: "Some 'er teeth, and some ain't."

"It's not a good story," he says about the name. "It just works. We sorta do this with all of our beer names. When [beer drinkers] really want to know the story or they come tell us, I just smile and say, 'Yeah.' There's multiple meanings. That's almost the beauty of a great beer name."

Sunshine Daydream

Fat Head's Brewery | www.fatheadsbeer.com

Fat Head's Brewery

Production brewery/tasting room:
17450 Engle Lake Drive
Middleburg Heights, Ohio 44130*
(216) 898-0242

Brewpub:
24581 Lorain Road
North Olmsted, Ohio 44070
(440) 801-1001

First brewed: 2013
Style: Specialty India pale ale
Alcohol content: 4.9 percent
IBUs: 60
Available: Year-round in bottles and on draft

IF YOU LIKE THIS BEER, here are five other Ohio craft beers to try:

- Land-Grant Greenskeeper
- Rhinegeist Zen
- Great Lakes Steady Rollin' Session IPA
- MadTree PSA
- The Brew Kettle All for One

*Opening November 2017

Sunshine Daydream

www.fatheadsbeer.com | Fat Head's Brewery

NO CRAFT BREWERY is immune to consumer trends, including Fat Head's. Co-owner and brewer Matt Cole, who has had tremendous success with Head Hunter IPA and Hop JuJu Imperial IPA, saw the response that Founders Brewing was having with its wildly popular All Day IPA, a 4.7 percent session beer.

With more craft beer drinkers gravitating toward session IPAs, Cole designed his own, calling it Sunshine Daydream. The 4.9 percent beer is bursting with hop aroma and flavor.

"The idea was to still have hop flavor and a good firm body but have a hop-forward presence," Cole says. "We put a lot of our emphasis on the tail end. We don't focus on making it extremely bitter for the sake of being bitter. It's more about the end of the boil and how we extract those hop flavors and aromas that carry over into the finish. It's a very hard balance to pull off, to be honest with you. It's really easy to make it too aggressive."

Cole loves the name, which he borrowed from the Grateful Dead song "Sunshine Daydream." Every Fat Head's beer label features a big fat guy. In the case of Sunshine Daydream, the fat guy has a braided ponytail and is giving the peace sign while wearing a tie-dye shirt. The beer also carries the tagline "Peace, Love, and Hoppiness." It's Cole's favorite label.

He believes session IPAs are here to stay and won't be a passing fancy for beer drinkers.

"They never stopped loving hoppy beers, but they were just looking for a hoppy beer that you could drink more of," he says. "You drink four Head Hunters, and you're pretty scoobered."

Total Eclipse Breakfast Stout

Maumee Bay Brewing Co. | www.mbaybrew.com

Maumee Bay Brewing Co.
27 Broadway St.
Toledo, Ohio 43604
(419) 243-1302

First brewed: 2009
Style: Stout
Alcohol content: 9.1 percent
IBUs: 30
Available: Year-round on draft and in bottles

IF YOU LIKE THIS BEER, here are five other Ohio craft beers to try:

- Zaftig BamBaLam
- Jackie O's Java the Stout
- R. Shea Polymer Caramel Espresso Stout
- BottleHouse Rising Star Coffee Stout
- Fat Head's Beam Me Up Imperial Coffee Stout

Total Eclipse Breakfast Stout

www.mbaybrew.com | Maumee Bay Brewing Co.

YOU'VE HEARD of garage bands? Maumee Bay Brewing's Total Eclipse Breakfast Stout started as a garage beer. Way back before Clint McLaughlin took over the production brewery at Maumee Bay, he was just a homebrewer who loved intense, high-alcohol stouts.

He and a buddy would spend way too much money at the local bottle shop on beers such as North Coast Old Rasputin, Three Floyds Dark Lord, and Founders KBS. Given the amount of cash flying out of their pockets, they figured they should make their own.

So they brewed—in the garage—a 9.1 percent beer featuring espresso beans and milk sugars. It was a knockout from that first batch.

"I remember thinking, 'This tastes like something I'd spend $10 for on a bomber,'" says McLaughlin, who has since left the brewery.

He opted to name his beer Total Eclipse because . . . well . . . if you hold it up to the sun, you're not going to see through it.

When McLaughlin started working at Maumee Bay, he brought the recipe with him. That recipe hasn't changed at all from that initial brew, but one ingredient's source has. Maumee Bay now uses local coffee roaster Flying Rhino.

Maumee Bay had a little fun with the beer label. It features a paper plate, which throws off some beer drinkers. What's a paper plate got to do with a big stout? It's more about the name Total Eclipse. The poor man's way to view an eclipse safely is to put a pinhole in a paper plate and use it to project the eclipse onto another surface. Some beer drinkers get the reference and find it funny; it flies over the heads of others.

Despite Total Eclipse's 9.1 percent alcohol, the beer doesn't taste boozy, thanks to the lactose providing a residual sweetness.

"We are constantly told that Total Eclipse is as good as or better than any coffee stout that's out there," brewery manager Craig Kerr says. "It stacks up against anybody."

Turbo Shandy

Hoppin' Frog Brewery | www.hoppinfrog.com

Hoppin' Frog Brewery
1680 E. Waterloo Road
Akron, Ohio 44306
(330) 352-4578

First brewed: 2009
Style: Fruit beer
Alcohol content: 7 percent
IBUs: 7.3
Available: Seasonally during the summer on draft and in bottles

IF YOU LIKE THIS BEER, here are five other Ohio craft beers to try:

- The Brew Kettle Sandy Shores
- Thirsty Dog Raspberry Ale
- Rocky River Blueberry Ale
- Rivertown Blueberry Lager
- R. Shea Orange Mango Shandy

Turbo Shandy

www.hoppinfrog.com | Hoppin' Frog Brewery

TURBO SHANDY owes its existence to Country Time Lemonade. Really. Hoppin' Frog Brewery owner and brewer Fred Karm and several friends were participating in an Iron Brewer competition in 2009 on a super-hot day. They wanted something light and easy to drink.

Enter "Frogweiser." That was the nickname for the brewery's Smashing Berry Ale before the berries were added. They decided to mix some Country Time Lemonade into pitchers of Frogweiser. It tasted so good that Karm was inspired: Why couldn't he make something like this?

"I knew my friends liked it a lot," Karm recalls, while chatting at the Hoppin' Frog Tasting Room. "And my friends don't realize it, but they're my guinea pigs."

He examined the lemonade's ingredients and concluded there really were just three: lemon, citric acid, and sugar. He figured he could create a shandy that duplicated that taste. And—voilà!—Turbo Shandy.

It certainly is a departure flavorwise for a brewery known for big beers like B.O.R.I.S the Crusher, Gangster Frog IPA, and Barrel-Aged Naked Evil Barley Wine. But Turbo Shandy stays true to the Hoppin' Frog mantra, offering a bold, intense flavor.

The seasonal beer—it's available only during the summer—has turned out to be so popular that Hoppin' Frog can't keep up with the demand. While Hoppin' Frog beers are distributed in 15 countries, Turbo Shandy is limited to Ohio because the brewery just can't make enough to serve other areas.

That said, beer geeks, those guys and gals who are so serious about their beers that they rank them on RateBeer.com and BeerAdvocate.com, aren't enamored with Turbo Shandy, handing out low scores for the brew. Karm jokes that if he stopped making it, perhaps his brewery would be ranked even higher overall. That's not going to happen, of course.

"I'm proud to be that open-minded," Karm says about his love of Turbo Shandy.

Uncle Rusty

Columbus Brewing Co. | www.columbusbrewing.com

Columbus Brewing Co.
2555 Harrison Road
Columbus, Ohio 43204
(614) 224-3626

First brewed: 2010
Style: Red India pale ale
Alcohol content: 8.5 percent
IBUs: 80
Awards: Gold medal at the 2014 World Beer Cup
Available: February to March on draft

IF YOU LIKE THIS BEER, here are five other Ohio craft beers to try:

• Fat Head's Bone Head Imperial Red Ale

• Barley's Ulysses Imperial Irish Red

• Great Lakes Nosferatu

• MadTree Un-Happy Amber

• Smokehouse Red Molly

Uncle Rusty

www.columbusbrewing.com | Columbus Brewing Co.

COLUMBUS BREWING owner and brewer Eric Bean laughs at the question: Who is Uncle Rusty? Bean isn't much for fanciful names when it comes to beer, so there must be some story behind the brewery's gold medal–winning imperial red ale. And, in fact, there is.

He admits that he's constantly asked about the name.

Uncle Rusty is a real dude named Rusty Jones. He's not Bean's real uncle, though.

"He worked for our old distributor," Bean says. "He's just that good-time guy who everybody likes. We always joked that he was Uncle Rusty."

Uncle Rusty—the beer, not the man—grew out of Columbus Brewing's Hop Odyssey program launched in 2010. Bean embarked on an ambitious effort to release a different hoppy small-batch beer each month.

When it came to making an imperial red ale, Bean wanted a high alcohol content and an intense caramel, toffee character. He's not a fan of regular ol' hoppy red ales, so he uses crazy amounts of crystal malts, balancing that with plenty of hop flavor and aroma. At 8.5 percent alcohol by volume, it's not a summer-sipping brew.

The Hop Odyssey ran for two years, with enough positive response for Uncle Rusty that it became a regular.

"It's such a nice-drinking beer," Bean says. "It's got all those complementary flavors. It's big. It has big malt undertones to it. But those hops just cut right through it. On the aromatics side of it, there are big grapefruit aromas from the hops to blend with those malts. It just works."

White Rajah

The Brew Kettle | www.thebrewkettle.com

The Brew Kettle
8377 Pearl Road
Strongsville, Ohio 44136
(440) 239-8788

First brewed: 2010
Style: India pale ale
Alcohol content: 6.8 percent
IBUs: 70
Awards: Gold medal and Best of Show at the 2011 International Beer Fest in Cleveland; bronze medal at the 2015 Great American Beer Festival
Available: Year-round on draft and in bottles

IF YOU LIKE THIS BEER, here are five other Ohio craft beers to try:

- Market Garden Citramax
- Fat Head's Head Hunter
- Fifty West Punch You in the EyePA
- Hoof Hearted Musk of the Minotaur
- Hoppin' Frog Hoppin' to Heaven IPA

White Rajah

www.thebrewkettle.com | The Brew Kettle

T HE BREW KETTLE head brewer Jack Kephart was tired of hearing about Fat Head's Head Hunter IPA this and Fat Head's Head Hunter IPA that. He was determined to make a true West Coast–style IPA to compete with the award-winning beer from the brewery down the road.

So Kephart, who has a great sense of humor, created White Rajah India Pale Ale. The name is significant, and it has nothing to do with the second-most-populous country in the world. See, the "White Rajahs" were a monarchy that ruled Sarawak on the island of Borneo for more than 100 years, starting in 1841. The family also just happened to outlaw headhunting.

Get it?

The beer even carries the tagline "Taming the Savage Hop." But don't worry, there's no bitterness between the brewers. It's just some friendly smack.

Kephart entered White Rajah in Fat Head's Celebration of the Hop competition, an annual judged contest to determine the best IPA. White Rajah won Best of Show that first year and again the next year. Head Hunter wasn't entered, by the way.

The beer also was declared the Best of Show at the inaugural International Beer Fest in Cleveland in 2011. IPA fans, especially those in the Cleveland area, love to debate which is their favorite: White Rajah or Head Hunter? There's even a Black Rajah, a black IPA.

"My whole goal in doing IPAs and double IPAs is to maximize hop flavor and aroma and minimize the bitterness as much as we can," Kephart says.

White Rajah—made with Citra hops, which give it a citrus and tropical fruit quality—has become The Brew Kettle's flagship beer. Kephart says White Rajah fans can expect the beer to evolve.

"It's going to change over time as new hop varieties come out," he says. "It's going to get tweaked and adjusted. I consider it a living beer."

Wooster New Stout

JAFB Wooster Brewery | www.jafbwooster.com

JAFB Wooster Brewery
120 Beall Ave.
Wooster, Ohio 44691
(330) 601-1827

First brewed: 2012
Style: Foreign stout
Alcohol content: 6.7 percent
IBUs: 50
Awards: Silver medal at the 2014
Great American Beer Festival
Available: Year-round on draft

**IF YOU LIKE THIS BEER, here are
five other Ohio craft stouts to try:**

• Seventh Son Black Sheep

• Zaftig Black Perle Stout

• Mt. Carmel Stout

• Millersburg State Route 39 Stout

• Masthead Stout

Wooster New Stout

www.jafbwooster.com | JAFB Wooster Brewery

WOOSTER NEW STOUT is not a milk stout or a dry stout or a sweet stout or a Russian imperial stout. It's a foreign-style stout, which happens to be one of owner-brewer Paul Fryman's favorite styles.

He got introduced to that style while serving as an assistant brewer at Great Adirondack Brewing in Lake Placid, New York, and he's loved it ever since.

"It's a big, hearty beer with a lot of roasted character, so it has a ton of flavor, but it's still drinkable," he says. "The finished product is extremely roasty. You get coffee notes out of it, even though there's not coffee malt or coffee in it. You get dark chocolate. It borders on that 'Is it dry? Is it sweet?' It's just a lovely beer. The finished product always puts a smile on my face."

He was smiling even wider when the beer won a silver medal at the 2014 Great American Beer Festival. Since then, Wooster New Stout has become one of the brewery and taproom's best sellers. Fryman says his customers get a little restless if they don't see it written on the beer chalkboard behind the bar.

What some beer drinkers may not realize is that Fryman bounces back and forth between using a British yeast and an American ale yeast. Most people can't tell the difference, but the British yeast version is a little sweeter.

Why does he do that? "Just to see," he says with a laugh, adding that the beer with the American ale yeast won the GABF medal.

As for the name, Fryman says it made him chuckle. The foreign style is an old one.

"I just thought it'd be funny to go against the grain and go with Wooster New Stout," he says.

Wulver Wee Heavy Ale

Thirsty Dog Brewing Co. | www.thirstydog.com

Thirsty Dog Brewing Co.
529 Grant St.
Akron, Ohio 44311
(330) 252-2739

First brewed: 2012
Style: Barrel-aged Scotch ale
Alcohol content: 12 percent
IBUs: 22
Available: November through February on draft and in bottles

IF YOU LIKE THIS BEER, here are five other Ohio craft beers to try:

- Millersburg Barrel Aged Doc's Scotch Ale
- Hoppin' Frog Barrel Aged B.O.R.I.S.
- Great Lakes Barrel-Aged Blackout Stout
- Warped Wing Barrel-Aged Whiskey Rebellion
- Jackie O's Bourbon Barrel Brick Kiln

Wulver Wee Heavy Ale

www.thirstydog.com | Thirsty Dog Brewing Co.

THIRSTY DOG BREWING'S OWNER John Najeway got inspired while visiting breweries throughout Europe during the fall of 2011. His stops included revered operations such as Cantillon and Liefmans, where he marveled at the open fermentation process and was particularly taken with how the breweries age their beers.

He returned to the United States determined that his Akron brewery would launch its own cellaring program, starting with two bourbon-barrel-aged beers.

He just had to figure out which ones. The award-winning Siberian Night Imperial Stout was an easy call to go into the Four Roses Bourbon barrels. Everybody barrel-ages stouts. But he and brewmaster Tim Rastetter also wanted to design a new beer, opting for a Scottish wee heavy, figuring it would be big and malty enough not to be overpowered by the bourbon.

"We designed *that* beer to work with *that* barrel," Najeway says.

Wulver sat in the barrels for three months before Najeway and Rastetter snuck a sample. It was beautiful. But they kept aging it. At six months, it was even better. And each subsequent taste was even more exquisite. The beer peaked at 11 months, picking up the perfect blend of wood and bourbon.

At 12 percent alcohol by volume, Wulver was the strongest beer produced by Thirsty Dog before Ohio did away with its alcohol limit for beer in 2016.

"It's a real sweet, balanced beer that works well with the bourbon barrel," Najeway says.

Thirsty Dog started selling 12-ounce bottles in 2013. Just like its fellow barrel-aged Siberian Night, Wulver comes in a black bottle with gold lettering on the label and a gold foil wrapper around the top to distinguish it from the rest of the Thirsty Dog lineup.

Wulver isn't an inexpensive brew, with a four-pack initially retailing for $23.99.

"It's pricey," Najeway admits, "but it's worth every penny."

COOLEST
**BREWERIES
TO VISIT**

Carillon Brewing Co.

www.carillonbrewingco.org

CARILLON BREWING Cº

Premium Ales & Hearty Fare

Hist. **DAYTON O.** 1850

Opened: 2014
Owner: Carillon Historical Park
Key beers: Porter and Coriander Ale

Carillon Brewing Co.
1000 Carillon Blvd.
Dayton, Ohio 45409
(937) 910-0722

BACK IN THE 1970s, Australian singer Peter Allen had a hit with the tune "Everything Old Is New Again." That could be the theme song for the Carillon Brewing Co.

Located on the grounds of the 65-acre Carillon Historical Park along the Miami River in Dayton, the brewpub recreates the brewing process and recipes from the 1850s. The brewers aren't using any modern shortcuts, either.

There's no computer-controlled brewhouse. There are no giant stainless-steel fermenters. And there's no machine to grind the malted barley.

Instead, a visitor is transported back in time. There's a brick, two-story, wood-fired, gravity-fed brewing system. There are hoists and pulleys to assist the brewers in getting grain to the top of the brewhouse and American oak barrels in which to age the beer.

Workers wear period costumes and even grind the barley by hand. So when Carillon says its beer is handcrafted, it really means it.

"There's no behind the scenes," says former brewmaster Tanya Brock, one of the few professional female brewers in Ohio. "When we say historical, every step of the process is historical."

The brewpub was the brainchild of

Brady Kress, Carillon president and chief executive officer, who was inspired by memories of his grandfather making wine in Dayton. He wanted to create an entertaining and educational brewery, where people could come to see and learn how beer was made in the nineteenth century.

He has succeeded.

The brewhouse and the workers are on full display, with no glass separating them from visitors. People can watch as the workers stoke the fire, roast barley over an open flame, and fill the barrels with wort.

As for those recipes, they searched brewers' historical documents, including housewives' journals, to find authentic recipes from the time. The first two beers were a coriander ale and a porter.

Carillon Brewing Co. brewmaster Tanya Brock works at the Dayton brewery. Carillon focuses on replicating brewing from the 1850s—right down to the period costumes. *Photo courtesy of Carillon Brewing Co.*

When it opened in late 2014, Carillon was considered the first brewery of its kind in the United States.

It's housed in an open, 10,500-square-foot brick building that was constructed new to look old. To complement the authenticity of the brewing process, the bricks, wood, style of windows, and nails were selected to match the era. Those strap hinges on the gigantic front doors were crafted by blacksmiths.

Carillon features a full-service restaurant, offering up fare such as potato and leek soup, roasted chicken, and Wiener schnitzel.

While Carillon strives for historical accuracy, the brewery does offer several modern conveniences. The brewpub sells glass growlers to go, and there's a gift shop where you can buy a T-shirt or other items. There also are modern restrooms, thank goodness.

Father John's Brewing Co.

www.fatherjohnsbrewery.net

FATHER JOHN'S†
HEAVENLY. DEVILISH BREWING COMPANY

Opened: 2013
Owner: Dr. John Trippy
Key beers:
St. Michael's Pale Ale and Dirty Monk Doppelbock

Father John's Brewing Co.
301 W. Butler St.
Bryan, Ohio 43506
(419) 633-1313

FATHER JOHN'S Brewing Co. is much more than a brewpub. It's a spiritual museum and, quite simply, a heavenly first for Ohio.

Father John's—a brewery, restaurant, and brew-on-premise operation—is located in a red-brick, former Methodist church that was built in the 1890s. The church, located just off the town square in Bryan, a city of about 8,500 people in the northwest corner of Ohio, was vacant and had fallen into disrepair before being bought by Dr. John Trippy, a retired maxillofacial surgeon and owner of Wild Winds Buffalo Preserve in nearby Fremont, Indiana.

Trippy had a vision to turn the church into a beer-themed tourist attraction akin to Church Brew Works, a famous brewery inside a former Catholic church in Pittsburgh. He purchased a six-kettle brewing system from The Brew Kettle in Strongsville, hoping to replicate the success of that brew-on-premise business in the Bryan community.

Unlike Church Brew Works, though, Father John's brewhouse isn't in the sanctuary.

Trippy, who invested more than $2 million in the project, built his brewery onto the back of the church. He added an expansive, serene outdoor beer garden, complete with paths and seating, then

surrounded the garden with a large stone wall, along one side of which rests a tombstone. Uncovered during the construction, the inscribed headstone bears the name of Minora Minger, a nine-year-old girl who died in 1903.

That tombstone wasn't the only interesting find. In the church basement, Trippy discovered a crypt, the final resting place for a former pastor. Instead of sealing it over, he installed a glass cover, to allow inquisitive people to peer in at the coffin, and turned the room into a separate, small dining area. It's called the Crypt Room.

The restaurant, which occupies the basement, serves plenty of bison from Trippy's farm.

Father John's Brewing in Bryan was the first brewery to open inside a former church in Ohio. Founder John Trippy has turned the brewpub into a religious museum filled with relics.

The sanctuary is reserved for community meetings and private gatherings, such as weddings. It features a massive, working pipe organ, spectacular leaded stained-glass windows, and a second-floor balcony. Trippy even restored the bell tower; now area residents can hear the bells peal once again.

A spiritual man, Trippy has filled the restaurant and beer garden with religious artifacts gathered during his journeys. Buddhist, Christian, Jewish, Hindu, Native American—a variety of spiritual beliefs is represented on every wall and around every corner, giving each room the feel of an art gallery.

"I really sense when you touch old things there's a spirit that you can feel," Trippy says about his hobby of collecting religious antiques.

The bar, made out of poured concrete, is shaped like a cross. Meanwhile, at the back of the bar, a statue of Buddha overlooks the restaurant. And a red hymnal rests on each table.

All this makes Father John's much more than just a place to grab a beer. Father John's is a religious experience.

Great Lakes Brewing Co.

www.greatlakesbrewing.com

Opened: 1988
Owners: Pat and Dan Conway
Key beers: Edmund Fitzgerald Porter, Christmas Ale, and Blackout Stout

Great Lakes Brewing Co.
2516 Market Ave.
Cleveland, Ohio 44113
(216) 771-4404

PAT CONWAY'S chest puffed up with pride. The cofounder of Great Lakes Brewing was reading an article in the *Cleveland Plain Dealer* right after NBA superstar LeBron James had announced he was leaving for the Miami Heat back in 2010. The entire region was depressed and angry to be losing its hometown hero. But the newspaper offered up a list of reasons why Cleveland should hold its head high. And right there, along with the world-renowned Cleveland Clinic and the Cleveland Orchestra, was Great Lakes.

"The buttons on my chest almost burst," Pat Conway says. "I went, 'Holy shit.'"

It should have come as no surprise. Great Lakes is a Cleveland institution. Since its founding in 1988 by Cleveland-area natives and brothers Pat and Dan Conway—who knew nothing at the time about operating a brewery—Great Lakes has grown into one of the most respected breweries in the country. Thanks to the popularity and quality of its brands such as Edmund Fitzgerald Porter, Christmas Ale, and Burning River Pale Ale, it has become one of the largest craft breweries in the nation, ranking 21st on the Brewers Association's list in 2016.

The Conways took over a former tavern in the sketchy Ohio City neighborhood, opened a brewpub with a seven-barrel

Great Lakes Brewing in Cleveland is Ohio's original craft brewery. The Cleveland brewpub remains a must-visit for any craft beer drinker.

brewing system, and created one of the city's biggest tourist destinations. Along the way, they helped turn the area into a popular residential and nightlife district and paved the way for fellow neighborhood breweries, including Market Garden, Nano Brew, Hansa, and Platform.

"It's gratifying to see that Great Lakes is a successful brewery, but it's also a successful business that has helped the neighborhood," Dan Conway says.

Thousands of people visit now to eat at the restaurant that prides itself on using locally produced foods; to sample pub-exclusive beers at the brewpub, which still employs the original brewing system; to wander through the visitor's center, which resembles an art gallery with displays highlighting the brewery's storied history; and to take a tour of the 75-barrel production brewery that rose across the street.

The brewpub is so famous that it even had a starring role on the long-running TV Land sitcom *Hot in Cleveland*. The producers used an exterior shot of Great Lakes, which sits on a brick, tree-lined street, for the setting of the characters' favorite watering hole.

Inside, the restaurant remains small and intimate. But visitors are quickly reminded about the award-winning beer, as framed medals from the

Great American Beer Festival and World Beer Cup hang on the wall near the entrance of the brewpub.

Before Great Lakes, the building housed a tavern frequented by legendary crime fighter Eliot Ness, who once served as Cleveland's safety director. Bullet holes in the tiger-mahogany bar and walls are rumored to have come from Ness's gun.

The Conways, who strive to be as environmentally friendly as possible, also created a beer garden with radiant heat from a giant fireplace for the cold Cleveland winters and a roof that can retract on warmer summer days. There are also small bars in the basement and on the second floor, where people can gather and drink.

Great Lakes is one of the few breweries in Ohio large enough to have its own gift shop. In addition to beer, the brewery sells everything from tap handles to glassware to posters to lip balm to logoed golf balls.

It's not unusual to see people loaded down with cases walking away from the shop.

Pat Conway believes there's a simple reason that people love visiting Great Lakes. It goes beyond the beer or the brewery's history. He credits the employees.

"You can have the most charming, inviting facility in the city—which I would argue *this* is—but the staff are so warm," he says. "All these wonderful people. There's a warmth here. It represents Cleveland so perfectly."

Maumee Bay Brewing Co.

www.mbaybrew.com

Opened: 1995
Owners: James and Patricia Appold
Key beers: Amarillo Brillo, Buckeye Premium Beer, and Total Eclipse Breakfast Stout

Maumee Bay Brewing Co.
27 Broadway St.
Toledo, Ohio 43604
(419) 243-1302

MAUMEE BAY BREWING CO. is a tourist destination for many reasons. There's the beer, of course. The brewpub, located in downtown Toledo, serves tasty beers such as Total Eclipse Breakfast Stout and Amarillo Brillo, an imperial India pale ale.

The facility itself is a pretty decent attraction, too. The brewpub and its 15-barrel system—there's also a larger 30-barrel production brewery located across the street—are housed in the historic Oliver House, a former hotel constructed in 1859 by Major William Oliver.

The massive brick complex, which sits along the Maumee River and is on the National Register of Historic Places, contains not only the brewpub but also a small café, a theater, an upscale steakhouse, a college beer bar, and even townhouses. And ghosts.

The hotel was used as an infirmary during the Spanish-American War, and workers believe the friendly ghosts—yes, they are cordial—are still hanging around from that time. One of the apparitions, known as "The Captain," appears in a soldier's uniform.

While the beer, historic building, and chance encounters with the otherworldly guests are reasons enough to visit, what

makes the brewery a one-of-a-kind destination in Ohio is its function as an unofficial Toledo beer museum. People can spend hours looking through the estimated 5,000 to 6,000 beer-related items on display, ranging from crowns to signs. Owners James and Patricia Appold have packed the Oliver House with a seemingly endless supply of breweriana. Not familiar with the term? It's used to describe all sorts of beer collectibles.

Maumee Bay Brewing operates both a brewpub and a production brewery. The brewpub has been turned into a museum honoring Toledo brewing history.

As soon as visitors walk into the building, they are greeted with breweriana. The entranceway features a wide staircase that winds up to the brewpub on the second floor; along the way, the brick walls are decorated with signs, posters, old advertising, bottles, and cans. Much of the memorabilia focuses on Buckeye Beer, the famous Toledo brand that was once made by the *defunct* Buckeye Brewing Company, not to be confused with the *modern-day* Buckeye Brewing Company in Cleveland.

There also are glass cases filled with bottles, steins, crowns, and openers. And all this is on display before the entrance to the brewpub, where visitors can gawk at more than 700 beer cans, such as Schmidt, Olde Frothingslosh, and Cinci Lager Beer, along with old-fashioned beer trays and an old brown beer bottle dating from the 1800s that was unearthed during a building renovation.

It's not unusual for people to stare at the beer cans and share stories about the cans they collected as kids or the beer they drank as adults. Brewery manager Craig Kerr sees that happen all the time. He also finds it fascinating himself to look at all the different label designs that were used to attract beer drinkers back then.

"It's funny how things change but they don't change," Kerr says about how current craft brewers are so focused on the designs of their labels and logos.

But that's not all. Maumee Bay also pays homage to all the former Toledo brewers with its Toledo Brewing Hall of Fame. Along one wall in the brewpub hang framed plaques celebrating 10 of the breweries from Toledo's past: Buckeye, City, Eagle, Finlay, Grasser & Brand, Home, Huebner, Koerber, Lubeck, and Toledo.

The Oliver House has plenty of nooks and crannies crammed with even more beer items. Nevertheless, the workers estimate that more than half the collection is in storage because there's not enough room to exhibit all the items.

Many people who visit are surprised and then pleased to find so much breweriana on display.

"Anyone who is a beer drinker will enjoy this," Kerr says.

Moerlein Lager House

www.moerleinlagerhouse.com

Opened: 2012
Owner: Greg Hardman
Key beers: Over-the-Rhine Ale, Zeppelin, and Barbarossa Double Dark Lager

Moerlein Lager House
115 Joe Nuxall Way
Cincinnati, Ohio 45202
(513) 421-2337

MOERLEIN LAGER HOUSE Chairman Greg Hardman knows every nook and cranny of the brewpub; every detail in every historical advertisement from the 1800s hanging on the walls; every brewer's face, including his own, in the giant mural honoring Cincinnati's brewing history; every framed black-and-white photo pulled from a training manual for the former Burger Brewing Co.; and every Christian Moerlein beer bottle, as in every design ever made, on display in the lobby.

Hardman can tell a story about every item and share why it has a home at the brewpub. He places his hand on a nondescript sandstone wall on the first floor and says there's a reason real sandstone was used in the construction.

Not only is the nearby Roebling Suspension Bridge made out of sandstone, but the bases of all the breweries in Over-the-Rhine, the city's historic brewing district where the Christian Moerlein production brewery sits, were made from sandstone.

The brewpub, with its ultramodern architecture, pays tribute to the community's rich brewing heritage in other ways—with the old Christian Moerlein advertisements and the original Schoenling sign that greeted people at the former

The Moerlein Lager House overlooks the Ohio River in Cincinnati. It is a modern marvel, filled with breweriana honoring Cincinnati brewing history.

Schoenling Brewing Co. Hardman, who has revived famous Cincinnati beer brands such as Little Kings, Hudepohl, and Burger, and is fond of honoring the community's former Beer Barons, would have it no other way.

"You know what I think makes the Moerlein Lager House special?" Hardman asks during a tour. "We celebrate the past while, at the same time, we celebrate the future of craft beer."

The brewpub's 15-barrel stainless-steel brewing system, on display behind glass at the front of the building, pumps out plenty of Christian Moerlein brands on draft. The brewpub also offers about 30 guest taps and more than 100 brands in bottles and cans, easily providing one of the largest beer selections in Cincinnati.

As visitors enter the building, they are greeted with the phrase "Through these doors pass the greatest beer connoisseurs and brewers of our time." The brewpub is also one of a few in Ohio with its own gift shop, where visitors can buy everything from a T-shirt to a baseball hat.

It's not just the beer selection or the breweriana that are attractions, though. The building itself is impressive. The two-story brewpub sits along the Ohio River in Smale Riverfront Park. Thanks to giant windows that span more than half the building, it offers spectacular views of the river; Roebling Suspension Bridge; and Paul Brown Stadium, home of the Cincinnati Bengals. Great American Ball Park, home of the Cincinnati Reds, sits next door—or, as Hardman puts it, you could flip a beer coaster and hit the ballpark.

For baseball junkies, the brewpub is on the site of the former Riverfront Stadium, where Pete Rose became baseball's all-time hits leader with hit 4,192. There is a plaque on the floor commemorating the nine-minute standing ovation he received.

The restaurant and brewery are LEEDs certified, meaning they are as environmentally friendly as possible. Hardman notes that the building has incorporated geothermal energy into the brewing process, pulling cold water from two nearby wells.

"This is a world-class facility in a world-class riverfront park," he says. "Nowhere else in the United States do you have this. Actually, I know of nowhere in the world you have this."

Mt. Carmel Brewing Co.

www.mtcarmelbrewingcompany.com

Opened: 2005
Owners: Mike and Kathleen Dewey
Key beers: Nut Brown Ale, Amber, and Blonde

**Mt. Carmel
Brewing Co.**
4362 Mt. Carmel
Tobasco Road
Mt. Carmel, Ohio
45244
(513) 240-2739

MT. CARMEL BREWING has a seriously homey feel. What other quality could it have? The brewery was launched in the basement of Mike and Kathleen Dewey's white farmhouse, the same one that appears on all the beer labels.

The brewery is no longer in the basement—it's in a building constructed onto the back of the house—and the Deweys no longer live there, as they did when they first launched Mt. Carmel. But the farmhouse remains an integral part of the business, now serving as the tasting room.

The kids' former playroom now holds a small four-seat bar with eight beers on draft. It also serves as the gift shop, selling everything from T-shirts to six-packs. And the entire first floor—the former kitchen, living room, and den—has been transformed into a tasting room. Make that tasting *rooms*. There's no mistaking that you're in a house as you walk from one room to the next. There is no other brewery and tasting room like it in Ohio.

The Deweys have added an outdoor patio with a fireplace and expanded the parking area. They also added an events center on the property next door.

But back in the beginning, Mike and Kathleen Dewey were just living in their brewery. Or their brewery was living with

MT.
CARMEL

BREWING COMPANY
CINCINNATI

NUT BROWN ALE

Mahogany IN COLOR
ENTERING WITH HINTS OF
MAPLE ❋ FOLLOWED BY A
ROASTED
HAZELNUT BODY
BALANCING *a* CLEAN MALTY FINISH

OG 1.058 SRM 18.1 IBU's 38 ABV 6%

MT. Carmel Brewing Company is a family owned
and operated brewery established in 2005. Production
grows at the same address where it began. In the
basement of this farmhouse built in 1926. The
home now furnishes a full scale production
brewery offering several all natural hand-crafted
beers in bottles and kegs. All, of course with our
pleasant touch of fanaticism. To learn more, visit
us at mtcarmelbrewingcompany.com or call us at
513-240-BREW(2739). Please enjoy responsibly
and thank you for your support!

Mike Dewey

Mike Dewey - Owner/Brewer

them—whichever way you want to look at it. At the time, Mt. Carmel was the only brewery operating in a house in Ohio, earning it the nickname "basement brewer" in the Cincinnati media. Each morning, Mike Dewey would wake up and head downstairs to the office. Not having to pay rent helped Mt. Carmel keep its overhead and prices down.

"What better way than to live at the brewery and coexist with it?" Mike Dewey says. "I didn't even have to drive to work. It was cool. It was the most difficult yet rewarding thing I've ever done."

The difficult part involved spending 17 hours a day, seven days a week, in the basement, brewing to keep up with demand. It was a lot of time away from his two small children. He recalls a time when he didn't leave the house for four days; he didn't see his kids during that time, either, because he was working so much.

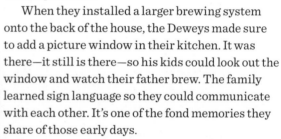

When they installed a larger brewing system onto the back of the house, the Deweys made sure to add a picture window in their kitchen. It was there—it still is there—so his kids could look out the window and watch their father brew. The family learned sign language so they could communicate with each other. It's one of the fond memories they share of those early days.

"They were always like, 'Making more beer,'" Mike Dewey says as he signs "Making more beer," which involves a rub down the right cheek near the chin.

Mt. Carmel is such a special place that Governor John Kasich came to the brewery in 2012 to tout a change in state law that allowed breweries to open tasting rooms without having to purchase a second costly license. The brewery also ended up on a video made by the Republican Governors Association, as the group promoted Kasich.

The Clermont County Convention and Visitors Bureau also has recognized its significance, touting Mt. Carmel on its website as one of the community's worthwhile tourist attractions right alongside places such as Kings Island, the Cincinnati Zoo and Botanical Garden, and the National Underground Railroad Freedom Center.

Mike Dewey laughs about how far the brewery has come from those difficult early days.

"It's insane," he says. "I know because I did it."

Mike and Kathleen Dewey launched Mt. Carmel Brewing in their white farmhouse. The brewery is still there, although the Deweys moved out long ago.

Old Firehouse Brewery

www.oldfirehousebrewery.com

Opened: 2014
Owners: Adam Cowan and Lori Ward
Key beers: Pin-Up Blonde Ale and Flash Point IPA

Old Firehouse Brewery
237 W. Main St.
Williamsburg, Ohio 45176
(513) 536-9071

THE OLD FIREHOUSE BREWERY isn't some chain place with fake firefighting memorabilia on display, designed to make you feel like you're inside a firehouse. It's the real deal.

The fire helmets and jackets hanging on the wall? Those are real. The fire extinguishers? Those are real. The giant garage doors in the front of the building that raise up? Those are real. The lime-green fire truck retrofitted to serve as a rolling beer truck? Well, of course that's real.

Old Firehouse Brewery sits in a former one-story fire station built in 1955 along West Main Street in downtown Williamsburg, a small village about a half-hour east of Cincinnati. Husband-and-wife owners Adam Cowan, a former firefighter and medical technician, and Lori Ward wanted their brewery to carry a firefighting theme and serve as a community gathering space that is both family- and dog-friendly.

"I was really able to keep the feel of a real firehouse because it was a firehouse," Cowan says. "I've said it, and it sounds hokey. The village built this building. Me and Lori, we own it, but this still belongs to the village."

The setting is so unusual that Old Firehouse even picked up a mention in the *USA Today* travel section in 2015 in a roundup of "the coolest converted buildings

The Old Firehouse Brewery operates out of—what else?—an old firehouse in Williamsburg. Owners Adam Cowan and Lori Ward have kept all the trappings of a fire station.

housing breweries." But it wasn't the first craft brewery to be located in an old firehouse in Ohio. The short-lived Firehouse Brewery occupied a fire station in Cleveland Heights in the mid-1990s.

Old Firehouse definitely plays up its roots, starting with the bar. The back of the small bar in the rear of the building resembles the back of a fire truck, thanks to the use of diamond plating found on the vehicles. The bar area also is filled with red beer mugs set aside for the regulars. What other color could they possibly be? There are firefighting posters with pithy sayings like "Firemen find 'em HOT and leave 'em WET," plenty of fire extinguishers on one of the walls, and an emergency light bar hanging from the ceiling.

Meanwhile, the 15-barrel brewing system and fermenters are in plain sight on the left side of the building as you enter. The only thing separating you from the brewing equipment is a fire hose acting as a rope barrier.

Not surprisingly, the beers feature firefighting names. There's Flash Point IPA, Hoser Gose, and Code 3 Red.

Then, there are those helmets and firefighting gear hanging on hooks along the right wall as you enter the building. The helmets and jackets aren't replicas. They are the real helmets and jackets worn by firefighters who worked at the station, including the gear used by the last chief, Richard Malott.

In all, there were 26 firefighters working there when the station closed in 1998. Cowan and Ward paid tribute to them by putting their names above their hooks and accepting donations of equipment.

"It's history," Cowan says about the display. "These were the guys who built this and kept this fire department going."

Put-in-Bay Brewery & Distillery

www.putinbaybrewery.com

Opened: 1996

Owners: Carl and Chris Krueger

Key beers:
Watermelon Wheat, West Shore IPA, and Pass Out Bourbon Stout

Put-in-Bay Brewery & Distillery
441 Catawba Ave.
Put-in-Bay, Ohio 43456
(419) 285-4677

NO ONE just pops in for a beer at the Put-in-Bay Brewery & Distillery. Well, maybe folks living on the island do. Yes, that's right—on the island.

Located on South Bass Island in Lake Erie, the brewpub is one of the most remote and difficult breweries to visit in the state, perhaps even in the entire country. See, you don't just drive up in your car. It's not that easy. Remember, it's on an island.

But getting there—whether it's by boat or plane—is half the fun. Once on the island, it's all fun.

The town of Put-in-Bay—the brewpub is named after its community—has a well-deserved reputation as a party destination. The downtown area is packed with bars and restaurants offering beer and drink specials; there also are a few wineries. With so many options available for booze, it's not out of the ordinary to see bachelor and bachelorette parties—or anybody else, for that matter—whooping it up on the weekends.

"It's a party island on Saturday," admits Carl Krueger, the cofounder and brewer at Put-in-Bay, one of three breweries on the Lake Erie Islands. The others are Kelleys Island Brewery on Kelleys Island and St. Hazards on Middle Bass Island. Neither Kelleys nor Middle Bass share the

Carl Krueger is the cofounder and brewer at Put-in-Bay Brewery & Distillery, a seasonal brewery on South Bass Island in Lake Erie.

celebratory notoriety of South Bass. Krueger is quick to point out that the rest of the week is great for families, and he advises those who enjoy a more mellow scene to avoid Saturdays. As someone who lives on the island year-round and raised two children there, he should know.

There are plenty of other recreational opportunities, such as swimming, fishing, biking, and sailing. And if history is your passion, then you'll want to visit Perry's Victory and International Peace Memorial, a 352-foot-tall tower built by the National Park Service to commemorate the Battle of Lake Erie, fought near the island during the War of 1812.

The red-brick Put-in-Bay brewpub, which once housed a fire station and sits next to the police department, sports an eight-and-a-half-barrel brewing system and serves casual food such as burgers, pizza, and chicken wings. The brewing equipment is located on the second floor, out of sight from visitors.

That wasn't always the case. For years, the brewery was located on the first floor, right where customers entered. But Put-in-Bay underwent a major renovation before the 2016 season. Yes, because it's on an island, the brewpub is a seasonal operation and open only from May through October. Tourists dry up when the weather turns cold and the lake freezes over.

That renovation included installing new lighting, a tin ceiling, and stones behind the bar to form a wall. The brewery also brought in new booths, placed new molding that was fashioned from local walnut trees around the bar, and bought new furniture.

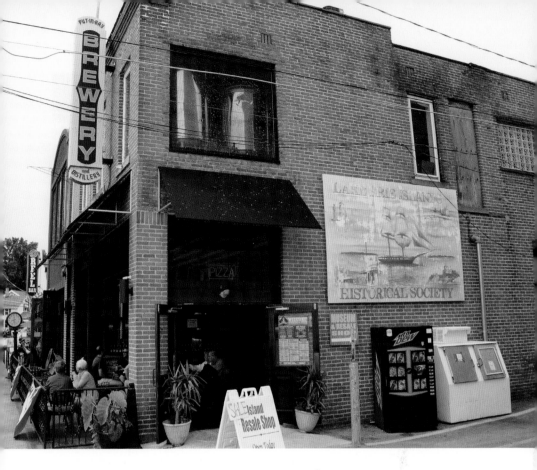

Krueger generally has six beers on draft at any given time. The most popular is a wheat called Summer Brew, although Krueger's personal favorite is the Pass Out Bourbon Stout. The Watermelon Wheat is a close second. That changes, come July, when Put-in-Bay celebrates "Christmas in July" with its Christmas Ale.

In addition to beer, Put-in-Bay offers its own spirits, thanks to a distillery on the first floor.

Put-in-Bay faces plenty of challenges when it comes to brewing. For starters, all the ingredients, from the hops to the malt, have to be shipped in by ferry. Krueger also freely admits that he uses malt extract as opposed to all-grain brewing, the common practice for professional brewers. It's just not feasible to dispose of used grain on the island, he says.

Another, perhaps less obvious, challenge is gauging how much beer to make. Because Put-in-Bay is a seasonal brewery, kegs left over at the season's end have to be dumped. Each year, it pains Krueger when he is forced to do that.

The brewpub doesn't distribute; to sample the beer, you have to visit.

Distribution, Krueger figures, would be too much of a hassle and would likely require setting up a year-round brewery off the island. And why in the world would he do that?

Craft breweries strive to become a destination for beer drinkers; Put-in-Bay is a tourist attraction already.

To get to the island, visitors who don't own their own boat or plane usually come aboard the Miller Boat Line, which offers a leisurely ride on one of its vehicle-passenger ferries, or the Jet Express, which provides a passenger-only trip. Either way, the boats offer beautiful views of the lake and islands, making the ride a significant part of the experience.

Most tourists opt not to bring their vehicles. Once on the island, people either walk or rent golf carts. As a result, South Bass is flooded with golf carts, with rented four- and six-seat Club Cars buzzing around.

Founded in 1996, Put-in-Bay Brewery & Distillery is one of the oldest craft breweries in the state. Over the years, Krueger has seen plenty of changes in his customers, concerning the consumption of craft beer.

"They are coming in for our beer now," he says. "In the beginning, it was a lot of Miller Lite and Bud Light. It's really done a 180."

Krueger also is happy to remain the owner of a small brewpub.

"I like the fact that everything we brew here is drank here," he says. "It's kinda neat. I don't need to distribute and all that stuff. I don't have any interest in it. I don't want to get too big. I like my winters off, and I get to travel and taste everybody else's beer."

Rhinegeist Brewery

www.rhinegeist.com

Opened: 2013
Owners: Bob Bonder
and Bryan Goulding
Key beers: Truth,
Cougar, and Saber
Tooth Tiger

Rhinegeist Brewery
1910 Elm St.
Cincinnati, Ohio 45202
(513) 381-1367

BRYANT GOULDING can hear the murmurs as first-time visitors to Rhinegeist Brewery walk up the dimly lit stairs to the production brewery and tasting room. People have to wind their way up a century-old black wrought-iron staircase, with gray concrete blocks on each side, to reach the brewery, located on the second floor of an immense red-brick building. That building once served as the bottling plant for the original incarnation of Christian Moerlein Brewing in Cincinnati's Over-the-Rhine neighborhood.

The climb is a little disconcerting that first time, given that visitors don't exactly know what they are getting into. Goulding, one of the co-owners, says he loves watching the reactions when people step out from the stairwell and into the brewery. Their mouths open in amazement, and they start slowly spinning around to take it all in.

It's no wonder. The space is open and massive. Unlike other large breweries in new industrial parks, the Rhinegeist building bears the scars of its manufacturing and historical past. Gray and blue concrete pillars rise to the 35-foot-high ceiling. Giant skylights welcome in natural light. Large murals are painted on the concrete walls. There are wooden picnic tables, cornhole games, and Ping-

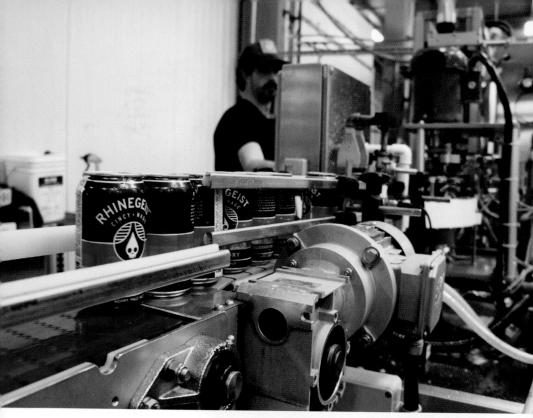

Rhinegeist Brewery is housed in a turn-of-the-century former bottling plant for Christian Moerlein Brewing. The Cincinnati brewery has become a must-stop for anyone interested in brewing history.

Pong tables. Two humongous industrial fans on the ceiling circulate air during the hot summer months. A small bar set in the northwest corner offers the obligatory craft beer chalkboard, letting drinkers know about the brews available that day. And, prominently placed, the stainless steel brewhouse, tank farm, and canning line are right out in the open for visitors to enjoy.

In 2015—a mere two years after opening—the brewery installed a new 60-barrel brewing system to keep up with demand for its popular brands such as Truth and Saber Tooth Tiger. It also opened a party space and a rooftop bar that provides spectacular views of the Cincinnati skyline.

Ohio features several craft breweries that have breathed life into old brewery buildings, including Thirsty Dog in the former Burkhardt site in Akron, Christian Moerlein in the former Kauffman facility in Cincinnati, and Portsmouth Brewing in a former brewery in that city. But none of them can match the immense and open layout of Rhinegeist.

"We're just really lucky," Goulding says. "You couldn't build a building like this today."

Rockmill Brewery

www.rockmillbrewery.com

**ROCKMILL
BREWERY**

Opened: 2010
Owner: Matthew Barbee
Key beers: Saison, Witbier, Dubbel, and Tripel

Rockmill Brewery
5705 Lithopolis Road NW
Lancaster, Ohio 43130
(740) 205-8076

Rockmill Tavern
503 S. Front St.
Columbus, Ohio 43215
(614) 732-4364

ROCKMILL BREWERY is a scenic postcard come to life. Located outside Lancaster along a country road and set among rolling hills, the brewery is housed on a former horse farm. There's beauty all around: natural, in the form of the Hocking River that meanders across the land; and manmade, in the form of a small white chapel that has become a favorite spot for weddings.

Rockmill Farms, as the property is known, is the perfect setting for a brewery that specializes in farmhouse ales, thanks to local water that is nearly identical in its mineral quality to that of Wallonia, Belgium, where the saison style originated.

"I was already excited about saison and farmhouse ale, and through studying it I realized how important the water was," owner Matthew Barbee says. "We had the water analyzed and, when the minerality came back from the lab, I was so excited because it was spot on."

Rockmill, because of its setting and its strict focus on Belgian-style ales, is a one-of-a-kind brewery in Ohio.

The 15-barrel brewhouse is located in the former stables, while the rustic farmhouse, replete with wood, serves as a warm, quaint tasting room. Artwork, much of it featuring horses, prominent in the Rockmill logo, decorates the walls.

Rockmill Brewery operates at a former horse farm outside Lancaster. The destination brewery features a horse on its logo.

A huge stone fireplace warms the main room, which opens onto a patio with a view of the chapel. And there's a small bar.

Barbee, who's passionate about creating Belgian-style ales, wanted to develop a gorgeous destination for beer travelers—one that would draw comparisons to wineries. Even his beer names—Saison, Witbier, Dubbel, and Tripel—are simple, named after beer styles, analogous to names given to wines. The bottles, available in both 750-ml and 375-ml sizes, feature corks and cages. His beer tastings also center around food, specifically cheese, charcuterie, and chocolate.

"We're very much into recreating that [winery] experience," Barbee says. "We hear a lot that this reminds me of Napa Valley or a winery tour in California, especially when the weather is warmer. I take it as a huge compliment. People are getting that kind of intimate type of experience while they are visiting."

He has announced plans to add a boutique hotel, restaurant, and larger brewhouse in order to accommodate bigger weddings and live music. Again, it's all part of his desire to develop a tourist destination that extends beyond brewing.

History is on his side. Rockmill Farms was an important post in the 1800s. At that time, the property served as a stopping point for travelers between New York and Kentucky. Next door was the Blue Ball Tavern and Inn, a popular resting place that still stands, now as a private residence. Down the street is Rock Mill Park, where visitors can tour a restored gristmill, originally built in 1824, and view the Rock Mill Covered Bridge, one of the iconic locations in Fairfield County.

COOLEST
BREWERY
NAMES

Bad Tom Smith Brewing Co.

www.badtomsmithbrewing.com

Opened: 2013
Owners: John Vojtush, Sheryl Gittins, and Sean Smith
Key beers: Breathitt County Blonde Ale, American Brown Ale, and American Outlaw Session IPA

Bad Tom Smith Brewing Co.
4720 Eastern Ave.
Cincinnati, Ohio 45226
(513) 871-4677

1836 W. 25th St.
Cleveland, Ohio 44113*

*Opening 2017

L ET'S GET this out of the way up front: Bad Tom Smith was a real guy—a real bad guy—who murdered people and terrorized eastern Kentucky in the late 1800s.

The day he was hanged in June 1895 in Jackson, Kentucky, an estimated 4,000 to 5,000 people showed up to see him off to the afterlife. Smith cemented his legend by being baptized the morning of his execution, confessing to his crimes, and eventually delivering a warning from the scaffold of the dangers of bad whiskey and bad women.

Then, according to the *Louisville Courier-Journal*, he asked the crowd to raise their hands as he spoke his final words: "Again I say to you, take warning from my fate and live better lives than I have lived. I die with no hard feelings toward anybody. There ain't a soul in the world that I hate. I love everybody. Farewell, until we meet again."

That story of sin and supposed last-minute redemption is why John Vojtush and his then-fiancée Sheryl Gittins bought the majority share of the Cincinnati brewery in 2015. The name Bad Tom resonates today in Kentucky, so they knew, if they could improve the quality of the beer, they had a winning brand. Many breweries have to manufacture a backstory or an

Bad Tom Smith Brewing in Cincinnati takes its name from an outlaw, Tom Smith, who was hanged in Kentucky in 1895. *Photo courtesy of Bad Tom Smith Brewing*

image; Bad Tom had no such problem. The brewery employs the slogan "Bad Ass in a Glass."

"Everything we do in the brewery—in terms of the names of our beers, a lot of our different marketing campaigns, the branding itself—is all tied to the Bad Tom Smith story," Vojtush says.

He cites, as an example, the fact that Breathitt County Blonde Ale was named after the county where Smith was hanged.

Not everyone is thrilled with the idea of a brewery being named after a murderer, and Bad Tom has received some criticism. But Vojtush, who's quick to point out that the brewery doesn't use blood or guns in its branding, says that, in general, people think "it's the coolest damn thing in craft beer."

The brewery, which upgraded to a 20-barrel brewing system in late 2016 and planned to open a location in Cleveland's Ohio City neighborhood, has

even brought in a professional actor who looks like Bad Tom to portray Smith at events.

Truth be told, the brewery didn't start out as Bad Tom Smith Brewing Co. The original owners had named it Double Barrel, but a trademark issue with another brewery of the same name sent them searching for an alternative.

Bad Tom Smith wasn't much of a leap. Cofounder Sean Smith is the great-great-grandson of Tom Smith's brother.

Vojtush loves sharing the story with customers. He enjoys watching their faces when they hear that Bad Tom isn't just some tall tale: there's a living link between the legend and the brewery.

"It's great to be able to sit down with patrons and strike up a conversation and talk about more than just this grain or that grain," he says. "We can talk about our brand."

Black Cloister Brewing Co.

www.blackcloister.com

Opened: 2015
Owners: Tom Schaeffer, Bob Hall, Mike Kennedy, and Scott Biddle
Key beers: Helles Angel, Marty Belgian Blonde, and Nature's Breast

Black Cloister Brewing Co.
619 Monroe St.
Toledo, Ohio 43604
(419) 214-1500

THE BLACK CLOISTER BREWING CO. owes its name to a religious maverick. Martin Luther, the theologian who was excommunicated from the Roman Catholic Church and launched the Protestant Reformation in the 1500s, lived in a converted monastery called the Black Cloister.

It was the perfect name for a Toledo brewery and tasting room that was started by a longtime Lutheran minister who just happened to have plenty of experience with beer. A certified beer judge, certified cicerone, and pastor of the Threshold Church, Tom Schaeffer cofounded the Glass City Mashers homebrew club, wrote a beer column for Examiner.com, and held combined beer tastings and Bible study in his living room.

"I would do an hour of formal beer tasting," he says. "Style study and so forth. It wasn't kidding around. It was really teaching about the beers. After we were done with the beer tasting, we'd study the Bible. As a consequence, my church is filled with a lot of beer geeks."

He punctuates that last line with a laugh. Those members of his congregation kept encouraging him to open his own brewery, which he did in early 2015, starting out in an old brick building downtown with a seven-barrel system.

Black Cloister Brewing in Toledo owes its name to Martin Luther, the leader of the Protestant Reformation. Luther and his wife, Katharina von Bora, lived in a building in Wittenberg, Germany, that was known as the Black Cloister.

As he searched for a suitable name that would reflect his steadfast belief that there is a connection between his faith and his work, a regional director with the Evangelical Lutheran Church of America suggested Black Cloister.

Even beyond the obvious tie with his Lutheran faith and Christianity's historical relationship with beer, the name worked on another level. Luther's wife, Katharina von Bora, a former nun, was a brewer. Black Cloister Katie Saison is named for her.

Schaeffer, who loves sharing the story behind the name, has carried over his faith into the brewery. There are plenty of religious references throughout the building, none more overt than the brewery's logo. It's a chalice with a cross inside.

Meanwhile, a giant mural runs the length of one of the walls and features the Four Horsemen of the Apocalypse from the book of Revelation, along with some head-scratching images like dinosaurs, the Death Star from *Star Wars*, and Castle Grayskull from *Masters of the Universe*.

There also is a framed portrait of Martin Luther. The original Black Cloister is now a museum called the Luther House in Wittenberg, Germany. Schaeffer wrote the museum a letter, telling the operators of his plans, and they sent back the portrait signed, "Best greetings from the original Black Cloister in Wittenberg, Germany."

But the religious theme goes well beyond how the brewery is decorated. The Black Cloister slogan, featured on coasters, is "Brew good. Do good." And Schaeffer built a clause into the operating agreement that requires 20 percent of the sales when the brewery starts distributing to go to ministry.

He adds that the Bible doesn't forbid alcohol, just drunkenness. It's all a matter of being responsible, he says.

"I actually find managing the taproom not that different from being a pastor, to be quite honest," Schaeffer says. "My job is to make people feel welcome. Greet new people. Listen to them. Give advice sometimes. These are all things I do on a regular basis anyway."

BREW GOOD.
DO GOOD.
-BCBC-

Butcher and the Brewer

www.butcherandthebrewer.com

Opened: 2014

Owners: Jason Workman, Chris Lieb, and Jeff Leonard

Key beers: Sticky Fingers DIPA, Stop Hop Kaboom, and Albino Stout

Butcher and the Brewer

2043 E. Fourth St.
Cleveland, Ohio 44115
(216) 331-0805

AS A KID GROWING UP in the immigrant-rich neighborhood around East 71st Street and Superior Avenue in Cleveland, Jason Workman recalls walking nearly every day with his grandmother Annabelle Rock to the local butcher shops.

The community was filled with them, representing all different nationalities. The quality of the meats found in those Croatian, Slovenian, and Hungarian shops far surpassed that of anything available at the grocery store.

So when Workman and his partners, Chris Lieb and Jeff Leonard—who also operate the craft beer haven Tremont Taphouse in Cleveland—were searching for a suitable name for their new brewpub on the city's fashionable, brick-paved East Fourth Street, it would seem that a butcher-related name was fate.

But the grandmother connection isn't the real origin of the Butcher and the Brewer name.

In another odd coincidence, Workman's brother Rex worked for years as a meat cutter in Cleveland and New York City. But having a real-life meat cutter in the family isn't the real reason behind the name, either.

The Butcher and the Brewer stemmed from a trip to the National Restaurant

Butcher and the Brewer in Cleveland was named appropriately. Not only does the brewpub house a brewery, but it also operates a butcher shop.

Association's annual conference in Chicago a few years before the brewpub opened. The partners had talked about starting a charcuterie program and were trying to come up with the ideal name to reflect that.

Walking down the street one day in the Windy City, Workman spotted a flyer for a hamburger and craft beer pairing. He can't remember exactly what the event was called, but it basically trumpeted an opportunity to meet a butcher and a brewer. And there's the real story.

"A lot of people think it's clever," Workman says.

The Butcher and the Brewer, which features a 10-barrel brewhouse, is known for more than just its beers. The brewpub also houses a full-service butcher shop and has a menu ranging from oysters to Lake Erie walleye to roasted chicken to fresh meats cut by Joshua Sampsell. The brewpub works with local farms and takes the whole animal. It also uses the whole animal, meaning there are different cuts and dishes available each day.

The brewpub also focuses on shared plates and has plenty of communal tables that almost resemble butcher blocks. The stainless-steel brewhouse gleams in the back of the brewery, technically named the Cleveland Brewing Co. The fermenters and bright tanks are all downstairs. Speaking of stairs, the wide stairwell leading up or down, depending on which way you're going, has the feel of an old-time subway station.

The bathrooms also are worth mentioning. There is a communal area to wash hands; private stalls for men and for women are provided on either side of the sinks. In other words, there's no private men's vs. women's room. (It's kind of a hoot to enter a stall to use a urinal.)

The name Butcher and the Brewer is a perfect fit because it reflects the brewery's artisanal craft in meat cutting and brewing.

"These guys are very skilled at what they do and they take their craft very seriously," Workman says. "And the final product that you get from somebody who has that kind of passion is awesome. That was the premise behind the Butcher and the Brewer. It's an Old World place. It's a throwback place to the artisans, to the tradesmen, to the craft."

Devil's Kettle Brewing

www.facebook.com/DevilsKettleBrewing

Opened: 2015
Owner: Cameron
Fuller
Key beers: Eric the
Red, Freak the Mild,
and Spider Silk

**Devil's Kettle
Brewing**
97 Columbus Road
Athens, Ohio 45701
(740) 589-7187

C AMERON FULLER wanted his brewery to have an aggressive name—even if that meant being a bit divisive.

"You want something that jumps out," he says. "I didn't want some bland name like the name of your town or the name of your street. . . . I didn't want a nondescript-sounding brewery, a forgettable name."

As he was trying to figure out that perfect brand for his 20-barrel production brewery and tasting room in Athens, Fuller stumbled across the story of the mysterious Devil's Kettle waterfall in Judge C. R. Magney State Park in Minnesota. A California-born nature lover who enjoys backpacking, he doesn't even remember how he heard about the place. He's never visited Minnesota.

Fuller was intrigued. The waterfall splits around volcanic rock, with half of the Brule River plunging 50 feet, then continuing on. The other half heads off into a pothole where the water disappears. Nobody seems to know where it goes.

Fuller started doing his research. There's a long history of religious names in Belgian brewing history and he couldn't believe that someone hadn't snapped up the waterfall name before.

Devil's Kettle Brewing opened in mid-2015, with Fuller doing much of the work

Devil's Kettle Brewing in Athens owes its name to a bizarre waterfall in Minnesota. Owner and brewer Cameron Fuller adopted the name but has never visited the site.

himself, including constructing the 25-foot bar out of nine different types of wood. An accomplished guitar maker, Fuller worked at guitar parts supplier Stewart-MacDonald in Athens for several years before launching his brewery. His aunt, an Ohio University professor, had landed him the job that brought him to Ohio.

He had been a homebrewer since his days in college when he bought his first Mr. Beer kit. In 2013, he won Best of Show in the Ohio Brew Week homebrewing competition.

"I was never one of those homebrewers who was satisfied with making a good enough beer or a drinkable beer," Fuller says. "I wanted to make a great beer. I learned the science behind it and understand what makes the difference between decent beer and great beer."

As for the Devil's Kettle theme, he could have featured a waterfall as the brewery's logo and brand. But he went with Beelzebub. It's fitting, given that Fuller enjoys heavy metal music and that's what plays over the sound system in the tasting room.

The brewery logo is a red kettle with the classic pointed devil's tail wrapping around it. One of his first beers was Pale Satan.

He admits that he hesitated at first in deciding whether Devil's Kettle was an appropriate name. He even ran it by some of his Christian homebrewing friends, who gave him their blessing.

"It's light-hearted," Fuller says. "We're not a church of Satan or anything."

Hairless Hare Brewery

www.hairlesshebrewery.com

Opened: 2013
Owners: Matt Harris and Mike Legg
Key beers: Rabbit Hole Imperial Chocolate Stout, Hoppin Hare IPA, and American Ale Belgian Blonde

Hairless Hare Brewery
738 W. National Road
Vandalia, Ohio 45377
(937) 387-6476

SURE, BOTH Matt Harris and Mike Legg are bald. Despite what some customers might think, that's not the reason their small brewery in a strip mall in Vandalia is called the Hairless Hare Brewery—one of the most unusual and coolest brewery names in Ohio.

The story behind Hairless Hare is a simple one that goes way back to high school in the 1980s, well before Harris and Legg lost their hair. That's when Matt Harris's brother Chris picked up the nickname "Hairless." It wasn't one of those cruel insults dreamt up by high school bullies. Instead, it was just funny. Chris kept his hair short, while all his friends embraced long hair and ponytails. His friends, playing off his last name, called him Hairless.

When Matt Harris made it into high school, he got the nickname "Little Hairless"—which he says he enjoyed. It was a little ironic, too, considering that Harris, at the time, had a big mane that could gain him entry into a hair-metal band.

Flash forward more than 20 years, and Harris and Legg were brewing on New Year's Eve 2012 and kicking around names for their new brewery. Harris offered up Hairless Hare. The next morning he launched the Hairless Hare Brewery

Both owners of the Hairless Hare Brewery in Vandalia are bald. But that's not the real reason for the brewery's name.

Facebook page, unbeknownst to his partner. There was no looking back.

"It's very catchy," Harris says. "It's easy to name beers. There are lots of places you can go with hairless and hare. And it kind of sounds medieval: Ye Olde Hairless Hare."

Many—but not all—of the Hairless Hare beers feature rabbit-related names such as Lepus IPA and Rabbit Hole Imperial Chocolate Stout. The Hairless Hare tap handles, made by Vandalia-based GO2 Technologies, are long metal bunny ears that easily stick out among the competition.

Hairless Hare opened in a small storefront in a strip mall. But Harris and Legg—thanks to regional demand for their brews—were planning to add a 20- or 30-barrel off-site production brewery. They also expanded their food options, which started with homemade pizzas.

The public response to the Hairless Hare name has been overwhelmingly positive. As soon as the brewery opened, Harris and Legg found a letter in the mail from a breweriana collector in Germany. He had seen the Hairless Hare name on the Internet and sent them a self-addressed stamped envelope, asking for any Hairless Hare swag they could send along.

They definitely enjoy the name.

"If you come in with too much hair, I charge you more," Harris says with a laugh.

Hoof Hearted Brewing

www.hoofheartedbrewing.com

Opened: 2012

Owners: Trevor Williams, Jarrod Bichon, and Ryan Bichon

Key beers: Musk of the Minotaur, South of Eleven, and Dragonsaddle

Hoof Hearted Brewing
300 County Road 26
Marengo, Ohio 43334
(419) 253-0000

Hoof Hearted Brew Pub & Kitchen
850 N. Fourth St.
Columbus, Ohio 43215
(614) 401-4033

TREVOR WILLIAMS worked for 10 years selling wine and encountered a lot of snobbery along the way. So when he and partners Jarrod Bichon and Ryan Bichon launched a brewery, he was determined to make sure there would be no airs with the business. It would be loose and fun.

"I said, 'Let's try to be the least pretentious brewery ever,'" Williams says.

That started with the name. A fan of heavy metal music and juvenile movies from the 1980s, Williams remembered a televised horse race from years ago, featuring a horse named Hoof Hearted. As the horse charged toward the finish line, the announcer began screaming, "Hoof Hearted," over and over. It was hilarious.

If you haven't caught on to the joke by now, Hoof Hearted sounds like "Who farted?"

It's one of the silliest, most ridiculous, and most irreverent names imaginable. Even though almost everyone advised them to dump it and they lost an investor who said there was no way he'd back a brewery named Hoof Hearted, the three partners ignored the naysayers. They even went one step further.

Their cartoony logo features a weird-looking centaur/satyr-like creature farting. They gave their beers weird names and

Hoof Hearted Brewing in Marengo has a lot of fun with its name and its brands. Say "Hoof Hearted" fast a few times; it sounds like "Who farted."

designed oddball artwork for them. There's Musk of the Minotaur IPA, Mom Jeans Milk Stout, Sidepipin', and Plutonium Nyborg.

"It tells you a lot about our operation," Williams says. "We never really thought of this as a super big, money-making venture. It was a passion project or a ridiculous expression and art project."

Hoof Hearted launched with a homemade 7-barrel brewhouse in rural Morrow County. It upgraded to a 15-barrel Tigpro system in 2015 and opened a tasting room. In 2016 it opened the Hoof Hearted Brew Pub and Kitchen at 850 N. Fourth St. in Columbus.

Despite the humorous name, Hoof Hearted has proven that it makes quality beer. The Musk of the Minotaur won a blind tasting in 2014 of the state's best IPAs and was crowned King of the Ohio IPA by a group of five Ohio beer blogs (including this writer).

"For the most part, 95 percent of people think it's awesome, hilarious," Williams says. "Every so often you'll meet someone who doesn't care for it. Well, you probably weren't going to drink our beer anyway."

JAFB Wooster Brewery

www.jafbwooster.com

Opened: 2012
Owner: Paul Fryman
Key beers: Wooster New Stout, JAF IPA, and Wayne County Cream Ale

JAFB Wooster Brewery
120 Beall Ave.
Wooster, Ohio 44691
(330) 601-1827

PAUL FRYMAN, his brother Tony Brown, and friend Mike West were sitting around trying to come up with a name for Fryman's new production brewery and tasting room in Wooster. Fryman and Brown had been going back and forth for a while, and then West finally blurted out, "It's just a fucking brewery."

He wasn't offering it up as a name. He was just expressing his thoughts about the endless debate. But something in that expression clicked because, well, his brewery would be just a fucking brewery.

Worried at first about offending the conservative Wooster community, which is home to the College of Wooster and the Ohio State University Agricultural Technical Institute, Fryman shortened it to JAFB, flipped the "F" backward, put the word "Wooster" in the name, and kept its real meaning on the QT. He still will hedge when some customers—at least those he thinks might not approve—ask what the name stands for, offering variations such as Join Attorneys for Beer, Just a Friendly Brewery, and Just a Family Brewery.

"I come from a really good family," says Fryman, who grew up nearby and cut his brewing teeth at the Great Adirondack Brewing and Snake River Brewing companies. "The 'F' word is not something that is thrown around by my mother or

JAFB Wooster Brewery owner and brewer Paul Fryman knows he could never spell out the JAFB. They stand for "Just a Fucking Brewery."

anything like that. I was kind of worried about that, and that's where the Wooster name came in. I just assumed that people would call it the Wooster Brewery. But nobody calls it that. They call it JAFB."

Most people start laughing when told the true meaning. Fryman recalls striding across the stage at the Great American Beer Festival in 2014 to accept a silver medal for his Wooster New Stout and Brewers Association director Paul Gatza shaking his hand and asking him about the name. Gatza thought it was hilarious.

But there is the occasional person who questions why Fryman, who also has won awards for his IPAs, would attach an offensive cuss word to his high-quality beers. He views that, in a way, as a compliment. The Wooster community has embraced the name as much as it has embraced the brewery, which occupies a brick building that once was used to manufacture buggies, surreys, and wagons. Fryman jokes that he should start a clothing line because so many people want to wear JAFB clothes. Here's where it gets weird: He gets plenty of requests for children's clothes.

As for the name, Fryman says he owes it all to West. And what did West get out of it? "He gets free beer," Fryman says, joking.

Toxic Brew Co.

www.toxicbrewcompany.com

Opened: 2013
Owner: Shane Juhl
Key beers: Porn or Pawn Pepper Pale Ale, ISO-Heaven IPA, and Abby XXXX

Toxic Brew Co.
431 E. Fifth St.
Dayton, Ohio 45402
(937) 985-3618

S HANE JUHL heard the complaints and concerns right away. Not many beverage companies would entertain naming their operation "Toxic" and creating a logo with a skull and crossbones—at least not any who wanted people to drink their beer without fear of keeling over.

The ruckus was so loud at first that Juhl thought about renaming the brewery and taproom, which opened in Dayton's historic Oregon District in 2013. But he couldn't bring himself to do it, knowing that the branding potential for T-shirts, hats, and other merchandise was off the charts.

"There's 5 percent of the people who hate the name and ask me why I'd ever be so stupid to name a brewery 'Toxic,'" Juhl says. "And there's 10 percent of people who fucking love it. They'll come here just because the name's Toxic. And there's the rest of the craft beer drinkers who just want to drink some beer and don't give a shit."

The name stems from his homebrewing days when he and his friends would extract caffeine from coffee beans using Everclear to create boozy concoctions. The liquid was strong and nasty to drink. Along the way, someone remarked that it was toxic. And there you have it.

The homebrewers branded themselves as the Toxic Brew Co., and when the time

came for Juhl to go professional, he stuck with the name. He knew he had something when he was out at Spinoza's Pizza and Salads one day and a woman asked him, "You're that Toxic guy, aren't you?" This was even before the brewery opened.

Right then, Juhl fully embraced the Toxic-guy identity and brand. He decided to dismiss the flak that he knew was coming. On top of that, he realized that people shop by labels and figured that the name Toxic Brew could help in the long run. One of the brewery's slogans is "Pick your poison."

There's certainly precedence in the craft beer industry for some offbeat and perhaps unappealing names. All you have to do is look at Rogue Ales and its Dead Guy Ale or Yellow Snow.

"You have to have a really thick skin in this industry," Juhl says.

Founder Shane Juhl says some people tried to talk him out of naming his brewery Toxic Brew Co.

Urban Artifact

www.artifactbeer.com

Opened: 2015
Owners: Bret Kollmann Baker, Scott Hand, and Scotty Hunter
Key beers: Phrenology Wild IPA, Sliderule, and Finn Berliner Pale Ale

Urban Artifact
1662 Blue Rock St.
Cincinnati, Ohio 45223
(513) 620-4729

B RET KOLLMANN BAKER, Scott Hand, and Scotty Hunter knew their brewery would be different, so they needed a special name to reflect the operation.

For starters, their brewery focuses exclusively on wild and tart ales, as opposed to classic American styles. It is housed in a former Catholic church built in 1873 in Cincinnati's Northside neighborhood—making Urban Artifact one of only a few Ohio breweries to repurpose a house of worship. And if that weren't enough to set it apart, their brewery also serves as a live music and performance venue.

So to recap: wild and tart ales; historic, spiritual setting; and music. It certainly should be easy to come up with a name that embodies the whole brand, right? Kollmann Baker, Hand, and Hunter set up a spreadsheet and kicked around hundreds of ideas, including Losantiville, Cincinnati's original name. With so many brewers having a hand in the kettle, so to speak, it wasn't easy finding a name that everyone agreed on.

"It made us really dig deep on how we saw the business not only starting out, but how it would shape up in the long term," Hunter says.

They chose Urban Artifact, a name that evokes almost an archeological aura, and

Urban Artifact focuses on wild ales. The Cincinnati brewery also is one of several in Ohio that operate in a former church.

promoted the slogan "Wild Culture" to project the essence of their beer. The name has been a major hit, as it works on multiple levels.

It captures the urban setting of the Cincinnati neighborhood, without being so local as to alienate outsiders. An urban style is reflected in the use of copper pipes for the tap handles in the tasting room.

Then there's the "artifact" aspect. That's a perfect descriptor not only for the religious site but also for the brewery's decision to revive many old beer styles that had largely disappeared. Urban Artifact launched with a Kentucky common, a gose, and a Berliner weisse. Those aren't exactly everyday styles served up at all neighborhood breweries.

"We're utilizing that Old-World technique of sour mashing and modernizing it with technological advancements that weren't available at the time," Hunter says.

The Urban Artifact tasting room is found in the basement of the stone church, where there is a small performance area. The 30-barrel brewing system is located in a separate building, formerly a school gymnasium. The sanctuary itself is used for shows and can be rented out as a reception space.

In the tasting room, wooden slats from the gym floor are used to hold

Urban Artifact is located in a former Catholic church built in 1873.

flights of beer, which are served in mini snifters. Those wooden slats also were installed behind the bar.

"We were going for an aesthetic we like to call industrial rustic," Hunter says. "You can definitely see that in our taproom."

Just as India pale ales exploded in popularity, Urban Artifact believes that sour, wild, and tart beers are the next defining movement in the craft beer industry. But they aren't just chasing a trend.

"Ultimately, they are the beers that we love to drink," Hunter says. "Everybody says that but you really have to believe it because you're selling them day in and day out. If I'm going to buy a beer, I'm not going to buy an IPA. I'm going to buy somebody's traditional sour or something that has Brett in it or something that's funky."

Zaftig Brewing Co.

www.drinkzaftig.com

Brewing Co.

Opened: 2013
Owners: Jason Blevins and Jim Gokenbach
Key beers: Juicy Lucy, BamBaLam, and Shadowed Mistress

Zaftig Brewing Co.
7020 Huntley Road
Columbus, Ohio 43229
(614) 636-2537

BRENT HALSEY still remembers the first time he heard the word. A high school English teacher who enjoyed uttering Yiddish words pulled out "zaftig" one day. Halsey chuckled at the pejorative connotation.

He doesn't remember exactly how the word was used by the teacher, but, given that zaftig refers to a woman with a plump figure, it likely wasn't meant as a compliment. Years later, Halsey and his wife ended up playing on a traveling Frisbee team named—you guessed it— Zaftig.

So when Halsey, Jason Blevins, and Jim Gokenbach decided to open a nanobrewery with plans to make big, bold beers with nothing less than 8 percent alcohol by volume, there was only one name that fit. It had to be the Zaftig Brewing Co.

"We always would seek out beers that we couldn't buy in Ohio," Halsey, who has since left the brewery, says about his homebrewing days with Gokenbach. "They were those big, full-bodied beers that we'd drive to Kentucky or Indiana or Michigan to pick up. When we were brewing, that's naturally the beers we would get into."

Zaftig operates with a three-barrel brewing system in a small industrial park just down the street from the gigantic Anheuser-Busch brewery in Columbus.

Zaftig Brewing in Columbus gets a lot of questions about its name. The term refers to a plump woman: a perfect fit for a brewery that wants to focus on full-bodied, high-alcohol brews.

Blevins and Gokenbach have plenty of fun with the Zaftig name and employ the slogan "Full-bodied ales." They've also come up with some creative names for their beers, such as Too Cans Imperial IPA and Shadowed Mistress.

So far, nobody seems offended. There even have been a few women who embodied the Zaftig name who claimed to enjoy it.

About half the customers seem to know what zaftig means, and only a handful of those will actually remark on it at the brewery. The owners think it's a hoot when beer drinkers come to the tasting room and share stories about doing an Internet search on the name at work. That's not recommended, though, because there are plenty of images of plump women that show up—many in various stages of undress.

"We're very open with the word, and customers really seem to like it," Gokenbach says.

10

INFLUENTIAL INDIVIDUALS IN THE OHIO **CRAFT BEER** INDUSTRY

Brad Clark

Brewmaster | Jackie O's Brewery | www.jackieos.com

FIVE OHIO CRAFT BEERS recommended by Brad Clark:

- Columbus Bodhi
- Fat Head's Head Hunter IPA
- The Brew Kettle White Rajah
- Thirsty Dog Siberian Night
- MadTree Lift

Jackie O's Brewery

Production brewery/ tasting room:
25 Campbell St.
Athens, Ohio 45701
(740) 447-9063

Brewpub:
24 W. Union St.
Athens, Ohio 45701
(740) 592-9686

JUST GIVE BEER A TRY. That's what Brad Clark—one of the most talented, creative, and prolific brewers in Ohio— thought as he was graduating in 2006 from Ohio University with a degree in creative writing. He wasn't sure what he was going to do with his future, but the Dublin, Ohio, native knew it likely didn't involve teaching or stringing sentences together for a living.

He had gotten hooked on craft beer while in college. While his peers might be guzzling the cheapest beer money could buy, Clark and his friends would grab six-packs of Great Lakes, Sierra Nevada, Pete's Wicked, Flying Dog, and Stoudts, just to try different brews.

He even started homebrewing twice a week, handing out his beer at parties. It was a way to relax and escape. He had found his lifelong passion.

Then an opportunity of a lifetime arose. Art Oestrike, who owned the Bagel Street Deli, decided to buy the O'Hooley's brewpub in Athens and asked Clark to stick around after graduation and become the brewer. He jumped at the chance to work at the newly minted Jackie O's Pub & Brewery and operate its seven-barrel system. Of course, he had no real experience with a professional brewhouse. His first all-grain batch—which happened to be Ohio Pale Ale—was made as a professional brewer.

Jackie O's Brewery brewmaster, Brad Clark, is considered one of the most creative brewers in Ohio. He has worked at Jackie O's since graduating from Ohio University.

"In the beginning, neither of us knew what we were doing," admits Clark, who's usually sporting a beard and wearing a green shorty cap emblazoned with the Jackie O's logo.

That all changed in late 2007. He attended the Siebel Institute of Technology in Chicago, and everything clicked. He started making big beers and barrel-aging them. He also began experimenting as much as he could, using locally raised pawpaws, honey, maple syrup, herbs, and walnuts, and putting an imperial stout in rum barrels. Actually, he was putting all kinds of beers in all kinds of barrels—brandy, chardonnay, sherry. It didn't matter.

Jackie O's went from this little, unknown brewpub in a college town to a worldwide beer sensation, racking up lavish reviews on RateBeer.com and BeerAdvocate.com. Jackie O's, which opened a production brewery in 2013 and started distributing across Ohio not only in cans but also in 375-ml bottles, is always represented among the top-rated beers from Ohio. RateBeer also has dubbed it as one of the best breweries in the world.

Clark's creativity is also demonstrated in his ability to produce an amazing number of styles. Jackie O's releases anywhere from 50 to 60 different brands a year, with 20 to 25 available on draft on any given day. In 2017, the brewery had more than 80 beers available for the celebration of its 11th anniversary.

Clark finds inspiration everywhere, particularly in music. He's a big Frank Zappa fan: Oil of Aphrodite and Grand Wazoo are a few of the beer names pulled from that musician.

"I can't imagine doing anything else," Clark says. "This is my career and I want to do it the rest of my life."

And lest you think he wasted his college degree, don't worry: Clark writes the stories and descriptions that appear on each beer label.

Matt Cole

Co-owner and Brewer | Fat Head's Brewery | www.fatheadsbeer.com

FIVE OHIO CRAFT BEERS recommended by Matt Cole:
- Hoppin' Frog D.O.R.I.S.
- Rockmill Saison
- Columbus Bodhi
- The Brew Kettle El Lupulo Libre
- JAFB Wooster New Stout

Fat Head's Brewery

Production brewery/ tasting room:
17450 Engle Lake Drive
Middleburg Heights, Ohio 44130*
(216) 898-0242

Brewpub:
24581 Lorain Road
North Olmsted, Ohio 44070
(440) 801-1001

*Opening November 2017

IT'S DIFFICULT to believe, but Matt Cole, the most award-winning brewer in Ohio, once had a serious case of self-doubt when it came to brewing. He felt he wasn't any good at it, or as he puts it, "I made shitty beer, man."

That was in his early days as a homebrewer, when he was attending the University of Pittsburgh and studying criminal justice. His homebrews were, to his taste, awful. He even considered giving up on the craft. That is, until Cole, who worked a sales job at Pennsylvania Brewing, attended the Siebel Institute of Technology in Chicago. The quality of his beer jumped after the training.

But he still lacked confidence. He apprenticed in Maryland at Baltimore Brewing, then moved to Ohio, where he brewed for about a year as an assistant at Great Lakes Brewing in Cleveland before latching on as the head brewer at Rocky River Brewing. It was there that Cole started to flourish.

The owners at Rocky River told him to keep a couple of lighter beers on tap at all times. Once they gave him that instruction, they allowed him the freedom to experiment. The quality of his beer jumped again, and he started winning medals at the Great American Beer Festival and the World Beer Cup.

Fat Head's Brewery brewmaster, Matt Cole, has been awarded more medals at major beer festivals than any other brewer in Ohio. He oversees beer quality at the Ohio locations in North Olmsted and Middleburg Heights and at the Portland, Oregon, brewery. *Photo courtesy of Matt Cole*

But Cole, who grew up in Ada, Ohio, still questioned his techniques. He took some trips to the West Coast and became friends with the brewers at Marin Brewing and Bear Republic Brewing. He quizzed them about how they brewed, particularly when it came to using hops.

"That's when I figured out how to make hoppy beer," says Cole, who's usually wearing an aging baseball cap. "Those guys sharing some of the knowledge that they accumulated over the years and then coming back and implementing it. There was a point where I would filter a lot of stuff, and I realized over time that filtration strips out a lot of color, body, mouthfeel, bitterness, and aromatics. I fine-tuned a little bit after sleeping on some Northern California couches. I was doing a little recon for awhile."

The quality of his beer jumped again. Then in 2009, he hooked up with some other partners and the Pittsburgh-based Fat Head's Saloon to open a Fat Head's Brewery & Saloon in the Cleveland suburb of North Olmsted. He has since partnered to open a Fat Head's production brewery in Middleburg Heights and a brewpub in Portland, Oregon.

Fat Head's—which has a logo featuring a big, fat guy's face—quickly became a popular spot for craft beer drinkers, especially after Cole won a silver medal at the Great American Beer Festival for Head Hunter IPA. That beer has won

numerous national awards since. Thanks also to his award-winning his Hop JuJu, an imperial IPA, Cole has earned a well-deserved reputation as one of the best brewers in the nation when it comes to the IPA style.

But Cole has proven again and again that he's skilled at making much more than just IPAs. He has won awards for fruit, wheat, porter, and smoke styles, too. When he travels to major beer competitions, he needs to take an extra suitcase—not for clothes or souvenirs, but for all the awards he brings home. Between 1998 and 2014, he took home an astonishing 28 medals from the Great American Beer Festival and the World Beer Cup.

Given his success, Cole is a much-sought-after brewer for collaborations. He uses those opportunities to engage in another passion of his—traveling. He's also a huge fan of hiking and outdoor activities. He created a special beer called Trail Head Pale Ale in 2013 to support the Cleveland Metroparks trail system. It should come as no surprise that the beer won a silver medal at the Great American Beer Festival that year.

When he travels, Cole usually pairs the trip with a beer-related visit, whether it's part of a trek to Germany or to the West Coast to hand-select his hops for the season. Those trips have made him a better brewer and inspired him to hone his craft.

"In this industry, you never stop learning," Cole says. "You need to befriend and network with people, and you can't be embarrassed by the fact that they know more than you do. I'm flattered when people say, 'You're the master of the hops.' I'm not the master of the hops. I learned along the way."

Pat and Dan Conway

Cofounders | Great Lakes Brewing Co. | www.greatlakesbrewing.com

FIVE OHIO CRAFT BEERS recommended by the Conways:

- Fat Head's Battle Axe Baltic Porter
- The Brew Kettle White Rajah
- Platform Esther
- Market Garden Pearl Street Wheat
- Brick and Barrel Bitter Chief

Great Lakes Brewing Co.
2516 Market Ave.
Cleveland, Ohio 44113
(216) 771-4404

IT WAS 1988 when a couple of brothers—one a schoolteacher and the other a commercial loan officer for a bank—opened a small brewpub named Great Lakes Brewing in Cleveland. Ohio's first microbrewery was born.

Pat and Dan Conway, two of nine children raised by an Irish Catholic family in suburban Rocky River, admittedly didn't know much about brewing at the time. They just knew, thanks to their experiences drinking in Europe while in college studying abroad, that they wanted to join the fledgling microbrew movement in the United States.

"We're trying all those beers in Europe and they were so much more flavorful and fresh than our effervescent, tasteless American lagers," Pat Conway says. "Why can't we have this in the United States? There was no reason. Seriously, back then it was coffee in cans, Wonder Bread, jug wine, and shitty American beer. We were on the forefront of that movement for boutique vineyards, craft beer, gourmet coffees, gourmet breads, chocolate.... This is a far more interesting culture than we had back in the sixties and seventies."

Of course, back when the Conways started, hardly anyone knew how to launch a small, independent brewery. In 1988, there were only 200 breweries scattered

Pat and Dan Conway, cofounders of Great Lakes Brewing in Cleveland, are credited with kicking off the craft beer movement in Ohio in 1988. Great Lakes is the largest craft brewery located solely in the state. *Photo courtesy of Great Lakes Brewing Company*

across the United States. As they sought help and advice, Pat Conway tells the humorous story about looking under "B" in the phone book for "brewer."

Boy, have things changed since. Today, there are thousands of breweries, including more than 200 in Ohio. Great Lakes—thanks to popular brands such as Edmund Fitzgerald Porter and Christmas Ale, and its sustainable business practices—has blossomed into one of the country's largest craft breweries, ranked by the Brewers Association as the 21st-biggest operation in the nation in 2016.

Along the way, the Conways have became legends in the industry alongside respected pioneers such as Ken Grossman of Sierra Nevada, Gary Fish of Deschutes Brewery, Jim Koch of Boston Beer, and Jeff Lebesch and Kim Jordan of New Belgium.

Together, they have built the company on a "Triple Bottom Line" philosophy—advocating their business practices, while often diverting credit to their employees, as much as promoting the beer itself. Great Lakes keeps a strong focus on economic, social, and environmental principles that aren't just talk. The company employs a "Fatty Wagon," a shuttle that repurposes vegetable oil used at the brewpub. It also operates its own farms, raising as much produce as it can at the Pint Size Farm at Hale Farm & Village in Bath Township and at the six-acre Ohio City Farm near its brewery.

Great Lakes also has organized the Burning River Fest every year since 2001. The music and environmental festival benefits the Burning River Foundation, a nonprofit group that supports local waterways. The company estimates that it has raised about $400,000 over the years for water conservation.

While the Conways refuse to chase brewery trends, they have been trendsetters. They are obsessed with quality and insisted on putting an "Enjoy by" date on their bottles. While some brewers will slap a date on the label that says when the beer was bottled, the Conways never thought that made sense for the average beer drinker. Great Lakes researched how long each of its brands remains fresh; that's the date that appears on the bottle, giving the consumer a hard freshness date.

The brewery also has inspired future brewery owners. Many brewers who worked at Great Lakes have gone on to launch their own operations, including Matt Cole at Fat Head's Brewery, Andy Tveekrem at Market Garden Brewery, and Dan Malz at Portside Distillery and Brewery.

Pat Conway, a graduate of Loyola University Chicago, has served as the public face of the company. He is, without a doubt, a major celebrity in Cleveland, having helped bring positive publicity to a city that often serves as the butt of jokes. He's a sought-after and entertaining speaker, with crowds gathering around wherever he talks.

He can just as easily share a funny story about how the brewery had to buy hundreds of gin shakers when it first started because there were no pint glasses available or talk with precision about how the brewery engaged archaeologists to recreate an authentic beer that would have been made in ancient Sumeria.

Meanwhile, Dan Conway has stayed mainly behind the scenes. But he is quite recognizable in his Westlake neighborhood on Christmas Eve. Every year, he delivers six-packs of Christmas Ale to his neighbors. He's up to handing out about 30 cases. He'll ring the doorbell and chat with the neighbor for a few minutes.

"I just wish them happy holidays or Merry Christmas," Dan Conway says. "If they're not home, we just leave the six-pack and keep going."

"I tried to do that but I took them all home and drank them," Pat Conway interjects with a hearty laugh. "I tried. I just got thirsty looking at them."

Rob Gerrity

Vice President of Operations for the Eastern United States |
Armadillo Insight | www.armadilloinsight.com

Armadillo Insight
20757 Anderson Road
Burlington, WA 98233
(360) 840-3313

ROB GERRITY figured that he would end up as a college professor, teaching art history somewhere. Although his career path didn't take him onto a campus full-time, he has become a teacher. He just traded subjects.

Gerrity, who lives in the Cleveland suburb of Rocky River, is vice president of operations for the eastern United States for Armadillo Insight, a data-processing company that consults with craft breweries, and is a former trade quality manager for Sierra Nevada Brewing. He also happens to be one of the country's foremost experts on beer quality. He writes the publications on the topic. As part of the Brewers Association's Draught Beer Quality subcommittee, Gerrity has helped produce the *Draught Beer Quality Manual* and *Draught Beer Quality for Retailers*.

The manuals are the bibles on draft beer technology for the industry, offering recommendations on everything from carbon dioxide pressure to how to properly clean glassware to tips for maintaining tap lines. While Gerrity goes unrecognized by the regular beer-drinking public, he has become a sought-after speaker at conferences and an adviser for bars and restaurants.

In other words, he teaches about beer.

"Beer freshness is the biggest problem

Rob Gerrity, who once oversaw quality operations for Sierra Nevada Brewery, has written pamphlets on draft beer quality for the Brewers Association. *Photo courtesy of Rob Gerrity*

that the whole industry faces, just because there are so many breweries and they make so many beers," Gerrity says over a beer at the Lizardville Beer Store and Whiskey Bar in suburban Akron. "Not everything is going to move through the system in a timely way."

He got interested in the topic while working at Great Lakes Brewing. He started at the Cleveland brewery as a tour guide when he was attending graduate school at Cleveland State University. During his downtime, he would read brewing books, work on the bottling line, clean kegs, and talk with the brewers, soaking up as much knowledge about the business as he could.

That led to an assistant brewing job; he eventually became the production manager for the brewery's 75-barrel production facility. But he found himself more intrigued by phone calls asking about beer freshness than by actual production. He recalls talking with customers who wanted to know why a Dortmunder they had at their neighborhood bar tasted different than the Dortmunder they had at Great Lakes.

"I became super interested in the postproduction quality aspect of what happens to beer after it leaves the brewery," Gerrity says. "I found that opportunity at Great Lakes, and I started looking at field quality as something that needed to be done. One of the only companies that was really doing that at the time was Guinness."

He left Great Lakes for Guinness; left Guinness for a sales job at Coors Brewing, where he learned the intricacies of the three-tiered selling system; then hooked on with Sierra Nevada. His position as trade quality manager involved overseeing the brewery's quality in 38 states. He estimated that he spent half his month traveling and educating everyone from his sales teams to distributors to retailers to allied industry companies on the proper ways to handle beer.

"Even though I discussed Sierra Nevada Brewing and things that separated Sierra Nevada from the pack, a lot of the big principles are not only good for Sierra Nevada, they're good for all beer," Gerrity says. "The concepts are good for Coors Light and Bigfoot and everything between. I feel like I'm a conservator of beer, and the educational piece is kind of the big umbrella. I concern myself with the condition of beer. I want to make sure the physical conditions and the storage and handling of beer is optimal for the consumer beer-tasting experience."

He left Sierra Nevada in 2016 to join Armadillo Insight, which analyzes data that help breweries with production, distribution, quality, and sales to big retailers.

Gerrity also laughs at the thought that he's still teaching, just not in the field he thought he would.

"I'm still an art historian, especially in the way I solve problems and see things from multiple points of view," Gerrity says. "I just focus on conservation of beer instead of conservation of paintings. For me it's a very logical analogy. Except that beer is more time sensitive than paintings are."

Greg Hardman

Owner | Christian Moerlein Brewing Co. | www.christianmoerlein.com
Chairman of the Moerlein Lager House | www.moerleinlagerhouse.com

FIVE OHIO CRAFT BEERS recommended by Greg Hardman:
- Columbus Creeper
- Fat Head's Hop JuJu
- Great Lakes Edmund Fitzgerald
- Weasel Boy Barrel Aged Anastasia
- Thirsty Dog 12 Dogs of Christmas

Christian Moerlein
1621 Moore St.
Cincinnati, Ohio 45202
(513) 827-6025

Moerlein Lager House
115 Joe Nuxall Way
Cincinnati, Ohio 45202
(513) 421-2337

FRESH OUT of Ohio University, Greg Hardman had two job opportunities: one with Xerox, the famous document company; the other with the Anheuser-Busch distributor in Athens, selling Cincinnati-regional brands like Burger Classic.

Hardman, who grew up in suburban Cleveland, chose beer, much to his mother's chagrin.

"She said, 'What in the world were you thinking?' I told her the truth. I told her I felt like I could be really good at selling beer," recalls Hardman, who's quick with a laugh. "I felt that it was something that I was passionate about."

It turns out that he is really good at it. And that passion, especially when it comes to Cincinnati's brewing history, has never wavered.

Hardman now heads both the Moerlein Lager House, a modern brewpub that sits along the Ohio River, and the Christian Moerlein production brewery, located in the former Kauffman Brewery in Cincinnati's Over-the-Rhine neighborhood. He has also been a major advocate for the city's Over-the-Rhine Brewery District Community Urban Redevelopment Corporation and the Brewing Heritage Trail, and his brewpub houses the Cincinnati Beer Barons Hall of Fame.

Greg Hardman is Cincinnati's newest beer baron. He oversees Christian Moerlein Brewing and the Moerlein Lager House. *Photo courtesy of Greg Hardman*

He has become—thanks to his buying up all of Cincinnati's famous beer brands such as Christian Moerlein, Burger, Hudepohl, and Little Kings—the community's latest beer baron, a distinction he proudly uses as his twitter handle: @CincyBeerBaron.

Hardman likes to talk about many key points in his life that influenced his career. That postcollege choice to pursue beer was the first. Many others, though, aren't necessarily happy memories.

He remembers being elated to receive an invitation to tour the Hudepohl brewery in Cincinnati in the mid-1980s because of his success in selling Burger Classic. But his excitement was short-lived.

His visit coincided with Hudepohl's merger with Schoenling Brewing. Hardman watched as some of the last bottles ever produced by Hudepohl rolled off the line at the facility.

He was also around when the last brewery-owned beer distributorship in Cincinnati was sold to a national competitor. And, later, he could only shake his head as those famous Cincinnati brands—ones he now owns—floundered in the rapidly changing beer industry. At one point, he had an opportunity to head the craft division at the Hudepohl-Schoenling brewery, but he saw that the company had no intention of throwing resources behind its best beers.

"I saw the demise happen literally in front of my face," Hardman says. "They had something that virtually no other city around the nation had. They had Yuengling in these brands, and they didn't realize it. They had Sam

Adams, and they didn't realize it. And they had unique brands like Little Kings. They had a brand for every category. I felt that if I ever had a chance to right that wrong, I would do something about it."

Hardman joined German beer company Warsteiner and rose through the ranks. Eventually, he became the president of its North American operations and opted to have the corporate headquarters relocated from Chicago to Cincinnati.

"All along I'm having this stellar frickin' career at Warsteiner and bringing them to be a top 20 import in the United States, and I'm looking like a hero," Hardman says. "But it bothered me in the back of my head. That statement: If I could ever right that wrong."

He even tried to convince his bosses at Warsteiner to invest in the Cincinnati brands, but they wanted him to focus on the German beer. Hardman bought Christian Moerlein in 2004, convinced he could revive the brand and make it relevant again. But then a funny thing happened.

When news broke that he had bought Christian Moerlein and planned to bring production back to the community, people pleaded with him to buy the other heritage brands as well. To the delight of many, Hardman bought the other brands, knowing that it would set him back from opening his own brewery.

"I felt the responsibility [to the community]," he says. "It was bigger than me."

Following the successful path of the Boston Beer Company and Brooklyn Brewery, Hardman had his beers produced out of state at first. Then in 2012, he opened the Moerlein Lager House and the Christian Moerlein production brewery. Many of his brands are now made, once again, in Cincinnati.

He also was a trailblazer when it came to the Over-the-Rhine neighborhood, where, back in the 1870s, 15 breweries had operated. Christian Moerlein was the first modern craft brewery to open there. Since then, Rhinegeist Brewery and Taft's Ale House have followed in the neighborhood, and the community's interest in craft beer has exploded.

"We feel we paved the way for a lot of that," Hardman says. "I really did this with the intention of bringing back Cincinnati's grand brewing traditions because I always felt it was a shame what happened to those brands. . . . It's about soul. Today we homogenize everything. When we lost our brewing heritage in Cincinnati, we lost our soul. We were a great beer center, and it's important to bring that back."

Craig Johnson and Matt King

Operators of Festivals Unlimited

Festivals Unlimited
P.O. Box 14564
Cincinnati, Ohio 45250
(888) 577-8881

T HE IDEA SPRANG from a simple conversation in a bar. Friends Craig Johnson and Matt King were chatting about beer festivals. They had attended a few. They knew about event planning. Why not launch their own?

That's how their company, Festivals Unlimited, and the Cincy Winter Beerfest were born. The first event, held in the ballroom at the Radisson Hotel in Covington, Kentucky, attracted 700 people. Johnson and King never looked back.

That was back in 2008, well before there was a festival, seemingly, every weekend, and well before the craft beer craze swelled in Ohio.

Now, the two Cincinnati natives are the undisputed beer festival heavyweights in Ohio.

While regular craft beer drinkers likely wouldn't recognize their names, they know of their work. Johnson and King run some of the biggest summer and winter beer festivals in the state, such as the Cincy Winter Beerfest, Columbus Winter and Summer Beerfests, Cleveland Winter and Summer Beerfests. They also put on events outside the state. Their festivals are held at the largest venues in Ohio: the Duke Energy, Cleveland, and Greater Columbus Convention Centers.

Craig Johnson *(right)* and Matt King run the biggest beer festivals in Ohio through their company, Festivals Unlimited. Their events are held in Cincinnati, Cleveland, and Columbus and in cities outside the Buckeye State.
Photo courtesy of Festivals Unlimited

In 2015, an estimated 85,000 people attended their events—not bad for a company that, at the time, didn't even have a permanent office. They used to work out of King's living room. They made that decision years ago while operating on a shoestring budget, figuring they'd rather not pump money into an office when they weren't certain how much money would be coming in.

"We had strong suspicions that it would be successful, but I don't even think we thought it would be as successful as it has gotten," says Johnson, who has served as the face of the festivals, while King works more behind the scenes.

Both college-educated men—Johnson has a degree in economics management from Ohio Wesleyan University, and King has a degree in communications and business management from Northern Kentucky University—believe their events prospered because of a winning formula. For starters, they pay for all the beer served, a move that the brewers obviously like. They also partnered with the Cincinnati nonprofit Big Joe Duskin Foundation,

Photo by Byronphoto.com

which supports music education and performances in schools. In 2014, they estimated their festivals provided about $160,000 for nonprofits, with the biggest share going to the Big Joe Duskin group.

Before launching the festivals, Johnson, an outgoing man who punctuates many of his comments with laughter, ran local bars like the Cock & Bull in Covington and put on events for MainStrasse Village. Meanwhile, King, who sports a ponytail and is more reserved, was a regular customer at Cock & Bull when the two hit it off.

They chuckle about how their beer festivals have changed since that first one held in a hotel ballroom. Back then, the festivals had about 30 participating breweries, offering 75 beers. Now, there are more than 350 beers. Back then, they had to convince their friends to come. Now, the events sell out. Back then, they relied on out-of-state breweries because the craft operations in Ohio were few and far between. Today, they put the spotlight on local brewers at each of their events.

They also take pride in helping, in a small way, to grow the craft beer industry by exposing drinkers to more breweries and styles.

"It's not a fad. Our festivals aren't a fad, and this whole movement isn't a fad," Johnson says.

"I guarantee there's a beer you will you find [at a festival], and you will like and be turned onto this revolution of flavor," King added.

Fred Karm

Owner and Brewer | Hoppin' Frog Brewery | www.hoppinfrog.com

Hoppin'
FROG
Brewery
Akron, Ohio

FIVE OHIO CRAFT BEERS recommended by Fred Karm:

- Listermann Nutcase Peanut Butter Porter

- Thirsty Dog Wulver

- The Brew Kettle White Rajah

- Thirsty Dog Siberian Night

- Great Lakes Barrel Aged Blackout Stout

Hoppin' Frog Brewery
1680 E. Waterloo Road
Akron, Ohio 33406
(330) 352-4578

IT'S THURSDAY NIGHT. So, naturally, Fred Karm is standing behind a turntable spinning rock records at the Hoppin' Frog Tasting Room. A huge music fan, Karm invested heavily in the 5,000-watt sound system, proudly pointing out the 32-channel mixer and 18-inch subwoofers.

On this particular day, the owner and brewer of one of the state's top breweries is featuring Rush, although he's open to recommendations from the hundreds of albums in his collection. Yes, that's albums. No cassettes or compact discs.

It's an appropriate scene, given that Karm is one of the brewing rock stars in Ohio and, arguably, the world. Through 2014, Karm had won 14 medals at the Great American Beer Festival and World Beer Cup, second in the state only to Matt Cole at Fat Head's Brewery. And he did that spanning employment at two breweries, proving his talent wasn't limited to just one operation.

Born in the Akron area, Karm attended the University of Akron and got a degree in electrical engineering. He took up homebrewing after college and excelled at it. He was so good that he was hired as the first brewer for Thirsty Dog Brewing, which started out as a chain of brewpubs. When those brewpubs shut down—the production brewery remains—Karm struck out on his own, opening the Hoppin' Frog Brewery in 2006.

His nickname growing up was "Frog," which helps explain the brewery name. How did he get that nickname? Well, his family wanted to avoid confusion because his father is also Fred Karm. Sitting at the taproom sampling a bottle of Frog's Hollow Double Pumpkin Ale, Karm prefers not to say precisely how he got the nickname, but he does joke that, growing up, he had an afro "you could lose pencils in."

Hoppin' Frog Brewery owner and brewer Fred Karm is considered a rock star in the craft beer industry. You can find him spinning records each week at the Akron brewery.

With his own brewery, Karm adopted an odd business model—at least, one odd for the time. Hoppin' Frog would produce only high-alcohol, high-flavor beers and sell them only in 22-ounce bottles. His brews also would command a premium price. At first, there would be no draft beer. To be successful, he knew he had to have wide distribution; he couldn't sell only in the Akron community.

That effort flew in the face of conventional wisdom, which called for breweries to offer draft beers and to build a loyal base in their backyard.

"I always wanted to make the beers that my friends wrote home about," Karm says. "And those were the strong beers. It was completely different from what an average brewery would do. . . . I knew I had to make the most killer beers that I could possibly make."

Eventually, Hoppin' Frog would offer draft beer, add a tasting room, and expand its distribution to 20 states and 15 foreign countries by 2015. The brewery is the only one in Ohio with regular foreign distribution. Hoppin' Frog is as well-known and respected in Europe as it is in the United States. So is Karm.

"I'm very proud of that," he says. "I never thought anything like that would ever happen. For people to appreciate my beer in these places that are the birthplaces of brewing like Belgium and Germany—I can't even fathom it."

John Lane

Co-owner of the Winking Lizard Tavern and the Lizardville Beer Store and Whiskey Bar chain | www.winkinglizard.com

FIVE OHIO CRAFT BEERS recommended by John Lane:

- Great Lakes Edmund Fitzgerald Porter
- Thirsty Dog Berliner Weisse
- Fat Head's Sunshine Daydream
- Columbus Bodhi
- Rockmill Saison

Winking Lizard Tavern and the Lizardville Beer Store and Whiskey Bar chain
25380 Miles Road
Bedford Heights, Ohio 44146
(216) 831-0022

JOHN LANE points to his messy office. There are six-packs and boxes of liquor on the floor. Beer books are stacked above his desk on a shelf. His walls are plastered with photos. Winking Lizard jackets are tossed across a chair. And paperwork is strewn all over his desk.

The co-owner of the Winking Lizard Tavern—a private chain that boasted 21 restaurants and bars and 1,200 employees scattered throughout northeast and central Ohio by 2015—is a busy man.

He's also arguably the most influential on-premise beer retailer and one of the most respected beer voices in the state, thanks to the volume of beer that flows through the Winking Lizard and Lizardville brands. That's evidenced by the fact that brewers and distributors from around the country descend upon the Winking Lizard in Bedford Heights each October for an annual gathering at which he talks about trends.

Lane speaks with authority, and the beer industry listens. The Winking Lizard, which is owned also by Jim Callam and Fred Kobzowicz, is a power in the industry: one of the top on-premise sellers of beer in the United States for Great Lakes Brewing, Dogfish Head Craft Ales, Stone Brewing, Duvel Moortgat, and Sierra Nevada. Every brewer wants to be sold there.

John Lane, co-owner of the Winking Lizard Tavern chain, runs the company's popular Tour of Beers program. Lane has been knighted by the Belgian Brewers Guild.
Photo courtesy of John Lane

But Lane hasn't always been in this position. He's a kid who grew up in the Akron area, drank Genesee Cream Ale in high school, and flew helicopters in the US Army. He admits he knew nothing about beer before joining his brother-in-law to open the second Winking Lizard in the 1980s. Even early on in his restaurant-bar career, despite overseeing the chain's popular Tour of Beers program, Lane had a blasé attitude toward beer.

That changed, though, thanks to two people: the late author Michael Jackson and Joe Waizmann, who used to be with Merchant du Vin and now co-owns Warped Wing Brewing in Dayton. Waizmann started educating him about Belgian beers, and Lane started reading Jackson's books. It was only in the early 1990s that he realized that, in the field of craft beers, an educated consumer becomes a loyal consumer, a beer drinker who discriminates.

"To do that, you have to be educated first," says Lane, who graduated from John Carroll University with a degree in political science and history. "I started reading whatever I could get my hands on. I have almost every beer book that was written back then. I love to read, and I love history, and it really fell in place."

He has become a huge proponent of quality and isn't afraid to share his opinions, which have included dumping some national brands and encouraging craft brewers to make low-alcohol beers so customers aren't afraid of having more than one at a sitting.

Today, he estimates that he samples anywhere from 500 to 600 beers a year to determine what to serve at the Winking Lizard and on the popular Tour of Beers program. He also makes trips to Europe to sample there. Those trips can be tiresome.

"Most people would say, 'Oh poor baby.' They all give the same reaction," Lane says with a laugh. "But it is hard work. At the end of the day, I'm keeping my eyes and ears open and trying to figure out what's that next cool thing to bring back to Ohio to share with everyone."

Interestingly, he's not a certified beer judge or a cicerone. But he is Sir John Lane. A huge proponent of Belgian beers, Lane was inducted into the Knights of Honor known as La Chevalerie du Fourquet des Brasseurs by the Belgian brewers guild in August 2012. The group honors people who have promoted Belgian beers in a positive way.

Lane, who counts Duvel and Orval as his favorite beers, calls it one of the highlights of his career.

"I'm very proud of that fact," Lane says. "An Ohio boy done good."

Mary MacDonald

Executive Director | Ohio Craft Brewers Association |
www.ohiocraftbeer.org

FIVE OHIO CRAFT BEERS recommended by Mary MacDonald:

- Columbus Bodhi
- Willoughby Peanut Butter Cup Coffee Porter
- MadTree Lift
- JAFB Wooster New Stout
- The Brew Kettle El Lupulo Libre

Mary MacDonald
Executive Director
Ohio Craft Brewers
Association
P. O. Box 8249
Columbus, Ohio 43201

MARY MACDONALD is a blur. It's the 2015 Winter Warmer Fest at Windows on the River in downtown Cleveland, and she's dashing from one area, one brewer, to the next, trying to ensure that the event is a success.

It's just another day in the life of the executive director of the Ohio Craft Brewers Association. MacDonald, who calls Columbus home, took over as the group's first full-time leader at the end of 2013, and she's been on the go ever since. Need proof? The first couple of years involved—take a breath because the list is impressive and long—wrangling together more than 100 craft breweries, developing a strategic plan, designing a new logo and branding, creating new beer festivals, launching the Ohio brewery magazine *On Tap*, and holding the inaugural Ohio Craft Brewers Conference and Trade Show.

Rabid Ohio State University fans might not want to hear this, but MacDonald looked to the state just north for help. The Michigan Brewers Guild, which has been around since 1997, offered plenty of inspiration and advice, especially when it came to running the organization and educational events.

But MacDonald was far from a beer rookie when she took over the association. While at Miami University in the early

Mary MacDonald serves as the executive director of the Ohio Craft Brewers Association. She oversees everything from memberships to beer festivals.

1990s, she studied abroad in Luxembourg, tending bar at a place called Pascha to earn some extra cash to travel around Europe. There, she sampled the more flavorful European brews, took in Oktoberfest in Germany, and drank Stella Artois in its home of Leuven, Belgium.

"Really, I was never a big Budweiser, Natural Light, Miller fan anyway when it came to beer, but living in Europe for a year, I became something of a beer snob with preferring imports," she says over lunch at Wolf's Ridge Brewing in Columbus.

Her first introduction to craft beer came thanks to Barley's Brewing, which opened in Columbus in 1992. She became somewhat of a regular at the brewpub.

MacDonald, who studied international studies and marketing in college, has an eclectic history. She worked for a while with the Elder-Beerman department store chain before buying a gallery and painting furniture in the Short North neighborhood in Columbus and later becoming the executive director of the Short North Business Association.

But owning the gallery, she says, didn't pay the bills, so she became the marketing director at North Market, the city's public market that houses independent food vendors and other merchants. While there, she recognized the emerging craft beer industry and, in 2006, launched North Market's inaugural beer festival, now called the Ohio Craft Beer Festival. The craft beer scene has been growing ever since in the state, and MacDonald sees no slowdown ahead.

"I hope that our existing breweries prosper, win fans and awards, and keep creating creative beers," she says. "I'd like for us to gain more recognition on a regional and national basis as a destination for craft beer. And I think that we will continue to see a proliferation of craft breweries, especially in smaller towns and communities."

Angelo Signorino Jr.

Head Brewer | Barley's Brewing Co. | www.barleysbrewing.com

FIVE OHIO CRAFT BEERS recommended by Angelo Signorino Jr.:

- Seventh Son American Strong Ale
- Columbus Creeper
- Columbus Bodhi
- Rhinegeist Saber Tooth Tiger
- JAFB Wooster New Stout

Barley's Brewing Co.
467 N. High St.
Columbus, Ohio 43215
(614) 228-2537

S ITTING IN one of the large wooden booths at Barley's Brewing in Columbus and sipping a pint of cask-conditioned Freshest Hop Available IPA—his favorite style—brewer Angelo Signorino Jr. admits he has nothing to complain about.

Signorino, an affable man with black glasses, short messy black hair, and a soul patch, is the longest-serving brewer at any single location in Ohio. He started at Barley's as an assistant brewer in 1992 and took over the reins when head brewer Scott Francis departed in early 2011.

Given the penchant for craft brewers to move around or strike out on their own, it's unusual that he is still brewing at the same location nearly a quarter of a century later.

"I'd like to think that it's just a good fit," Signorino says. "I really like having what I'd call artistic freedom here with the pub model. I can do things on a whim. It keeps things interesting and there are so many great people around me."

But it's not just his longevity that sets him apart from many of his peers. Signorino also pulled double brewing duty for years, serving as the head brewer at nearby Smokehouse Brewing, which was Barley's Smokehouse before a split of the operations. That arrangement ended in late 2014.

Angelo Signorino Jr.
is the longest-serving
brewer at any brewery in
Ohio. He has worked at
Barley's Brewing Co. in
Columbus since 1992.

Signorino began his brewing career like most professional brewers—at home. He recalls pooling birthday money from both his grandmothers in 1991 to buy a beer-making kit from the Winemaker's Shop, which was operated by Francis and his wife, Nina. He made a Bass Ale clone and fell in love with the process.

At the time, Signorino was studying anthropology at the Ohio State University and working at a grocery store. He gave that up to work at the Winemaker's Shop, then followed Francis when Barley's opened. He's never looked back or regretted his decision.

An avid bike rider, Signorino gets inspired about beer while riding. He not only bikes to work, but also used to make the three-mile trek between Barley's and Smokehouse on his bicycle. He confesses that he sometimes takes the long way. Some people may get great ideas while in the shower. Signorino gets them while riding.

Asked about the favorite beers he's made throughout his career, he cites two: Auld Curiosity Ale, an old ale, and Infinity Grand Cru, a Belgian-style dark strong ale.

He cannot imagine not working at a brewery.

"I love the physically demanding part of being a brewer," Signorino says. "And it's really hard for me to imagine not being able to do that physically demanding part. But if it came down to it and I just had an office and a clipboard and put on my boots sometimes, I'd still always want to be a brewer. It's mind-boggling to think of a career change. It's such a good fit. It involves so many things that I love. I love food. And beer to me is a special kind of food."

10

OHIO
FOODS
PAIRED WITH
AN OHIO
CRAFT
BEER

Buckeyes

Anthony-Thomas Candy Co. | www.anthony-thomas.com

Anthony-Thomas Candy Co.
1777 Arlingate Lane
Columbus, Ohio 43228
(877) 226-3921

SO WHAT exactly is a buckeye? To many Ohioans, it's the mascot for and name of the Ohio State University sports teams. It's also a great way to describe anyone from the Buckeye State.

To an arborist, though, it's a tree—the state tree of Ohio, in fact. The term is often used to describe the oval-shaped nut produced by the tree. That buckeye is toxic, so there's no reason to pop it in your mouth. But there is a tasty buckeye that you do want to devour, the candy version made of chocolate and peanut butter and designed to resemble the original.

Anthony-Thomas Candy Co. in Columbus has been making them since 1999. Today, the company, which was started in 1952 by father and son Anthony and Tom Zanetos, produces several million a year. Buckeyes are its best-selling candy.

They are sold in an assortment of box sizes, anywhere from a 6-piece package to a 60-count "Buckeye Dispenser." The company even has a 235-pound buckeye on display at its retail shop, priced at $3,500.

"Who can refuse chocolate and peanut butter?" asks Ross Fillmore, who provides tours at the Anthony-Thomas factory. "Unless you have a peanut allergy, it is a very popular combination."

Making buckeyes is pretty simple. In the old days—or even in kitchens around the

Buckeyes burst with peanut butter and chocolate flavor. They go perfectly with stouts such as Wolf's Ridge Dire Wolf Imperial Stout.

state today—you'd just roll balls of peanut butter and dip them into chocolate, leaving some of the peanut butter exposed to mirror the buckeye.

It's not that difficult at the factory level, either, but with one major difference. The process starts by adding a bit of white chocolate that duplicates the color of peanut butter to a mold. Then milk chocolate is added, leaving a hollow cup. The peanut butter is squirted inside, and the buckeye is sealed. Unlike the homemade versions, mass-produced buckeyes must encase the peanut butter in chocolate; otherwise, the candy will dry out or go stale.

Buckeyes are popular in Ohio for a variety of reasons. Thanks to the state's nickname, they are seen as an Ohio candy. Many people also remember their mothers and grandmothers making them. Then, there's that overriding connection with Ohio State. Recognizing the absolute passion and obsession of many Ohio State fans, Anthony-Thomas licensed the Ohio State logo to use on some of its candy boxes.

Not surprisingly, Anthony-Thomas has noticed that the sales of buckeyes are influenced by how well the Ohio State Buckeyes football team performs.

"We sell them all year round, but when the team is doing better, the sales are definitely better," Fillmore says.

Cincinnati Chili

Gold Star Chili | www.goldstarchili.com

WHAT TO DRINK WITH GOLD STAR CINCINNATI CHILI: Cincinnati chili has a sweetness to it, thanks to the cinnamon and Mediterranean spices. **Hudepohl Amber,** made by Christian Moerlein Brewing in Cincinnati, offers the perfect pairing because the beer won't overwhelm the flavor of the chili.

Gold Star Chili
650 Lunken Park Drive
Cincinnati, Ohio 45226
(800) 643-0465

BUFFALO HAS its famous chicken wings. Philadelphia has its cheesesteaks. And Chicago has its deep-dish pizza. All those foods became so popular that they slowly crept across the country to be enjoyed by millions outside their communities.

But Cincinnati's most celebrated food? Well, that has remained largely anchored in the Queen City.

Cincinnati chili is a meat-based sauce that's served over hot dogs or spaghetti, often with a heaping of grated cheddar cheese, onions, and beans. Don't confuse the sauce with traditional chili or spaghetti sauce, though. The recipe includes cinnamon and other Mediterranean spices.

Ever since brothers Tom and John Kiradjieff started serving up the dish on hot dogs in their Empress restaurant in 1922, Cincinnati chili has been a hugely popular food in the community. Today, there are about 250 chili parlors and restaurants in the region, with the most popular brands being Gold Star Chili and Skyline Chili. Cincinnati chili, estimated in 2014 to be a $250 million industry, helps drive the local economy.

"We like to think of Cincinnati as Chili Town USA," says Charlie Howard, vice president of marketing and brand development at the family-run Gold Star

Cincinnati is known for its signature chili, particularly from Gold Star Chili and Skyline Chili. Here, Gold Star Chili pairs well with Hudepohl Amber. *Photo courtesy of Gold Star Chili*

Chili, founded in 1965. "There are more chili parlors and chili restaurants here than any other city in the country. It's really the hometown food, and it's a part of the culture."

While other communities may have a CVS or Walgreens on every other corner, there's a Gold Star, Skyline, or other chili parlor seemingly on every block in Cincinnati.

Howard travels quite a bit for work and is always fascinated by the reaction when people learn he's from Cincinnati. They often mention Pete Rose, the all-time hits leader in Major League Baseball and former Cincinnati Reds player and manager. Then, they talk about that "funny chili."

There's also a funny way of ordering it. You don't just order the spaghetti dish. You order it in a certain way. There's two-way, spaghetti topped with chili; or three-way, spaghetti topped with chili and cheese; or four-way, spaghetti topped with chili, cheese, and onions or beans; or five-way, spaghetti topped with chili, cheese, onions, and beans.

Both Gold Star and Skyline offer catering now, and their brands are available in grocery stores as well as at their parlors. Gold Star even launched a food truck and often gets requests to be at wedding receptions.

"It's literally everywhere in this town in all kinds of forms," Howard says. "It's ubiquitous."

Cincinnatians are fiercely loyal to their favorite brand. Generally, they line up in either the Gold Star or the Skyline camp. It's sort of like cola when it comes to Coke vs. Pepsi or toothpaste with Colgate vs. Crest.

And don't mess with Cincinnati chili. In 2013, the website Deadspin ranked the dish as the worst regional food in the United States, calling it diarrhea sludge. To say the least, the community wasn't too fond of that ranking.

One member of the media even noted that Deadspin had made an enemy of the city.

Goetta

Eckerlin Meats | www.eckerlinmeats.com

Eckerlin Meats
116 West Elder Street
Cincinnati, Ohio 45202
(513) 721-5743

ECKERLIN MEATS knows a thing or two about goetta. Heck, the family-owned butcher shop, located at Cincinnati's historic Findlay Market, has been making the breakfast sausage since 1852. The shop advertises itself as "Old Fashioned Butchers. World Famous Goetta."

Eckerlin, which produces more than 25,000 pounds of the stuff each year, can back up its bold claim, having been named the best goetta by *Cincinnati Magazine* three times.

So what is it? *First things first.* It's not pronounced *go-ET-ta*. If you say it like that, you will surely be recognized as someone unfamiliar with Cincinnati and northern Kentucky. It's *GET-uh*, and it's a quintessential local food right up there alongside Cincinnati chili. The breakfast sausage is made with pork or, sometimes, beef, onions, pinhead or steel-cut oats, and spices. The meal, which is closely related to scrapple, dates back to the days of early German immigrants.

"When meat was rationed, everybody was looking for another meat alternative," says Josh Lillis, part of the sixth generation of the Lillis family who have worked at Eckerlin. "When they were butchering their pigs and cows, anything that didn't have fur or a bone on it went into the goetta pot."

Eckerlin Meats, a family-owned butcher shop in Cincinnati, has been making goetta, a breakfast sausage, since 1852.

Back then, that included organs. Today, Eckerlin uses just shoulders and chuck steak to create a brownish rectangular loaf, making 25 pounds at a time. The small shop will slice off a piece and fry it up in a pan right there for customers.

Goetta has an oat-and-smoke flavor and a nutty texture. Thanks to the oats and cuts of meat, the Eckerlin goetta is considered a low-fat, high-fiber food. Some people will eat it with maple syrup or jelly. Then, there's the good old goetta and scrambled eggs.

"If your parents ate goetta when you were growing up, you kinda eat goetta now," Lillis says. "It's one of those generation things handed down."

Eckerlin is far from the only goetta maker in town. Because of the dish's popularity, many restaurants produce their own version. Glier's Goetta across the Ohio River in Covington, Kentucky, makes it commercially for sale at stores. There also are two festivals held each year to honor the food: the Original Goettafest in Covington and Glier's Goettafest in Newport, where you can taste concoctions such as goetta Reubens and goetta pizza.

Jones' Marcelled Potato Chips

Jones' Potato Chip Co. | www.joneschips.com

Jones' Potato Chip Co.
823 Bowman St.
Mansfield, Ohio 44903
(419) 529-9424

THREE POTATO CHIPS sit on Bob Jones' desk. The president of the family-owned Jones' Potato Chip Co. in Mansfield keeps them because they are so rare.

One has little burned areas that form a smiley face. Another has little burned areas that create a frownie face. It's the last one, though, that really illustrates the family's relationship—and all of Ohio's relationship, really—with potato chips. It has a hole in the center in the perfect shape of a heart.

"I'm glad our family does this," says Bob Jones, who has worked at the business since the late 1970s and took over as president in 1996. "What we do makes people happy. Ball games, picnics, parties, and family gatherings—our product is consumed when people are having a good time—or drinking beer."

Ohioans love their potato chips, especially regional brands. The state is full of them. In fact, Ohio has the second-most potato chip manufacturers in the nation; only Pennsylvania is ahead of the Buckeye State. There's Grippo's in Cincinnati, Ballreich in Tiffin, Mikesells in Dayton, Shearer's in Massillon, Conn's in Zanesville, Gold'N Krisp in Massillon, and Corell's in Beach City. Frito-Lay and Herr's also operate plants in the state.

Jones' Potato Chip Co. dates to 1941.

Ohio is filled with regional potato chip manufacturers. Jones' Potato Chip Co. has been operating in Mansfield since 1941. Its marcelled chips go well with Phoenix Brewing's 5 Guinea ESB.

Bob Jones holds one of the three rare potato chips that rest on his desk. The heart shape illustrates his family's (and Ohio's) love of potato chips.

That's when Frederick Jones, after years of working as a food distributor and as a salesman for other potato chip companies, launched his own operation with a small kettle that produced anywhere from 10 to 12 pounds of chips a day.

He focused exclusively on marcelled chips. What are marcelled chips? Marcelled is just a fancy word for wavy. Frederick Jones saw it as a way to distinguish his chips from others.

His business timing wasn't great, though, considering he started the company just months before the attack on Pearl Harbor, which sparked World War II. He left the business behind and enlisted in the US Coast Guard.

Four years later, he returned to Mansfield to relaunch the operation. Jones' Potato Chip Co. now proudly proclaims that it's been around since 1945. It truly has been a family business, with Bob Jones estimating that about 40 family members and three generations of Joneses have worked at the company over the years.

Frederick Jones built his business on a specific blueprint of using quality ingredients, focusing on customer service, charging a fair price, and always acting ethically. It's a formula that has worked for the company through the years.

Now operating a few miles from where it first started in a white building on Bowman Street north of downtown, the business produces nearly 3 million chips a year. It also makes many brands on contract and has expanded into potato sticks, which in 2015 had grown into 50 percent of the business.

Jones' products can be found all over the country, thanks to its contract business, but the Jones' brand potato chips are sold mainly in a 40- to 50-mile radius around Mansfield.

And while the company for decades made just that marcelled style, it now makes an original style and a rippled chip, in all sorts of flavors, such as sour cream and onion and barbeque. It also uses different oils, soybean and corn, which impart distinct flavors. Bob Jones is partial to the marcelled style. Why wouldn't he be? He grew up with a can of those wavy chips always available at the house.

The marcelled ones also remain a favorite in the Mansfield area, where families grew up munching on Jones' chips at parties, while watching sporting events together, and on other special occasions.

"Wherever you were raised, whatever chips were in that community is probably what your favorite is," Bob Jones says. "There becomes an emotional bond that you don't even notice. It's very difficult to have that connection with very many products."

Mid's Homestyle Pasta Sauce

Mid's | www.mids.com

Mid's
620 N. Main St.
Navarre, Ohio 44662
(888) 879-6437

MID'S HOMESTYLE PASTA SAUCE doesn't spend a lot of money on advertising. The company is not on television or on the radio. It has a simple marketing strategy: once people taste its premium sauces, whether it's the best-selling Meatless, the Italian Sausage, or any of the other varieties, they won't go back to their previous brand.

"It's the way we make it," says Tom Bonk, director of plant operations. "It truly is homemade."

Mid's, located in Navarre, a small village of about 2,000 people in Stark County, got its start back in the late 1930s. That's when Mideo Octavio, whose nickname was Mid, emigrated from Sicily to the Canton area. He brought with him his mother's pasta sauce recipe—a family secret, of course—and opened a restaurant in Wilmot.

The eatery proved popular, but not as popular as the sauce. Octavio never wanted to waste any of the fresh sauce that was made daily. At the end of the night, people would come armed with their own pans and jars for him to fill up. That led him to open Mid's in the 1950s. The sauce became a regional favorite, thanks to the use of only fresh ingredients and to Octavio's reputation for simmering the sauces in an open kettle for four hours, an eternity in the industry.

Spaghetti fans all over the country know about Mid's in Navarre. The pasta sauce pairs well with lighter beers that won't overpower the flavor, such as Canton Brewing's Tuscora Pilsner.

Navarre is often filled with the scent of warm, fresh pasta sauce. Just down the street, there's also a Nickles Bakery. Village residents regularly are treated to the welcoming aroma of fresh sauce and bread.

For decades, the company would cook its sauces and brown its meat by hand, using wooden paddles; even the jars were filled by hand. R. Scott Ricketts and Steve Cress bought the company in 1997. Eventually they automated some of the processes in their 18,000-square-foot plant along the village's North Main Street. But, knowing what makes Mid's special, they haven't touched the original recipe or messed with the four-hour simmering time.

Ricketts recalls buying new simmering kettles that came with lids, which, if closed, could drastically cut down on the cooking time. The first thing he did was run out to buy chains to lock the lids in place so they could never be shut.

"Mideo started this, and he knew more about cooking pasta sauce than I do," Ricketts says, explaining why the company has remained true to its roots.

That philosophy has paid off. Mid's was strictly a regional product when Ricketts and Cress took over; the sauces were sold in about 80 stores. By 2014, Mid's produced 4.5 million jars, with distribution in more than 30 states. The sauce was available in an estimated 7,000 stores, including some of the nation's most popular and largest chains: Wegmans, Publix, Kroger, and Giant Eagle.

The company now offers 10 varieties: Traditional Meatless; Meat; Italian Sausage; Italian Sausage and Peppers; Tomato Basil; Meat and Mushroom; Extra Thick and Chunky; Mushrooms and Roasted Garlic; Three Cheese; and Garlic and Onion. It also sells pizza sauce. And while competitors have shrunk the size of their jars over the years, Mid's still sells a 32-ounce size because it wants to be different.

Despite the widespread availability of Mid's, the company routinely fields calls from people who can't find the sauces in their local stores. Every day, workers head to the UPS store to fill special shipping orders for fans. Ricketts admits that the attention is flattering and helps drive the company's desire to expand and eventually be sold nationwide.

The bottom line, Bonk says, is that Mid's knows people are busy today and don't have the time to make their own homemade sauce.

"We're doing it for them," he says.

Pierogies

Perla Homemade Delights | www.perlapierogies.com

Perla Homemade Delights
5380 State Road
Parma, Ohio 44134
(216) 741-9222

PIEROGIES ARE a versatile treat. The semicircular dumplings, which hail from Eastern Europe, can be—and are—filled with all kinds of foods. The traditional pierogi contains mashed potato and cheese, but the treat comes in other popular flavors, such as sauerkraut, mushroom and meat, sweet cabbage, prune, apple, and strawberry.

Yes, pierogies can be filled with fruit. But that's not all. The fillings are limited only by your imagination. Want lobster? *No problem.* Want pizza? *No problem.* Want something weird? *No problem.*

Perla Homemade Delights, an ethnic bakery located in a small shopping plaza along State Road in the Cleveland suburb of Parma, is more than happy to produce custom-made dumplings. The shop, run by the Serban family from the Transylvania region of Romania since 2006, has produced a special black-bean-and-cheddar pierogi for a wedding. They've also done vegan, pulled pork, and—what else would you expect on St. Patrick's Day?—corned beef, swiss cheese, and sauerkraut versions.

"That's what's cool about pierogies," says David Serban, who runs the distribution side of the business along with his brother Daniel. "You can make them for every niche, every person, every market."

Perla produces between 1,800 and

Perla Homemade Delights produces all kinds of pierogies by hand at its small shop in Parma. The BottleHouse Brewery in Cleveland Heights sells three different flavors. Here, their FlaschenHaus Kolsch is paired with potato-and-cheddar pierogies; Bike to Work Pale Ale with the jalapeño flavor; and Rising Star Stout with the cheddar-and-bacon.

4,800 pierogies a day. And each one is hand-pinched by one of a small group of workers, including matriarch Ana Edidia Serban, in the back of the retail shop.

Perla sells them to the public at the bakery and to restaurants, including the BottleHouse Brewery in Cleveland Heights, where they are a staple on the dinner menu. They are also available online; Perla fills orders from around the country.

In addition to a seemingly endless number of filling possibilities, there appear to be a million different ways to prepare pierogies, depending on your particular taste. Some people boil them. Some pan-fry them with oil or butter. Some grill them. Some deep-fry them. Some just cook them in the oven. David Serban has even thrown them on a George Forman Grill. A pierogi is a quick and easy meal.

Pierogies originated in Eastern Europe as a hearty peasant food—not surprising, given the basic ingredients of dough, potato, and cheese. Those original pierogies featured a sweet farmer's cheese, a variety that Perla still makes. For decades, the food has remained popular in the United States, thanks to immigrants, but that popularity has largely been limited to big cities in the Northeast.

"Our ultimate goal is to make pierogies a very, very popular comfort food for all Americans to enjoy," David Serban says. "The West Coast, southern United States —they don't even know what pierogies are. I have to explain them. Even southern Ohio— sometimes they don't know."

So how does he explain a pierogi to people unfamiliar with the food? It's just a pocket of dough filled with potatoes, vegetables, meat, or fruit, he says. All cultures seem to have their own version of pierogies. Italians have raviolis. The Spanish have empanadas. And the Chinese have pot stickers.

David Serban, who is partial to the potato, cheese, and bacon and the potato, cheese, and jalapeño varieties, says he still remembers his first taste of pierogies.

"It was really awesome," he says. "I like mashed potatoes. I like cheese. I like fried dough. So what is there not to like?"

Sauerkraut Balls

Ascot Valley Foods | www.ascotvalleyfoods.com

WHAT TO DRINK WITH SAUERKRAUT BALLS:
Sauerkraut balls feature an interesting combination of flavors thanks to the mix of ham, sauerkraut, and seasonings. Thirsty Dog Brewing's **Twisted Kilt Scottish Export Ale** is a great pairing.

Ascot Valley Foods
205 Ascot Parkway
Cuyahoga Falls, Ohio
44223
(330) 376-9411

KEITH KROPP is quick to point out that sauerkraut balls aren't an Ohio delicacy. They aren't even a northeast Ohio sensation. They are an Akron phenomenon.

"I always say it's like Buffalo wings to Buffalo. It's Philly sandwiches to Philly," says Kropp, chief executive officer of Cuyahoga Falls–based Ascot Valley Foods, which has been making sauerkraut balls for more than 50 years. "When people come in from out of town, Akronites say, 'You have to try these sauerkraut balls.' It's amazing the following they have in this region."

So what is a sauerkraut ball? It's a deep-fried ball of breading containing sauerkraut, ham, and a blend of seasonings.

Ascot Valley Foods makes a couple of different kinds, which are sold at retail locations and in bars and restaurants. There's the Bunny B variety, which contains ham, sauerkraut, beef base, Worcestershire and soy sauces, and seasonings. The Connoisseur ball comes with ham, sauerkraut, mustard, Tabasco sauce, smoke flavoring, and seasonings. Then there are the Habaneros, which feature habanero pepper flakes. Fans usually dip the balls in sauces, such as ranch and Thousand Island dressings, or in mustard.

"Some people raise their nose at

Sauerkraut balls are a regional treat in Akron. Ascot Valley Foods produces them for restaurants, bars, and retailers. The food pairs well with Thirsty Dog Brewing's Twisted Kilt Scottish Export Ale.

sauerkraut and don't like sauerkraut," Ascot Valley Foods Chief Operating Officer Joe Rogers says. "But when they eat the ball, people love it."

Innovative foods... Always in good taste

He noted that he, himself, has family members who don't enjoy sauerkraut, but they eat the sauerkraut balls because of the ham and other flavors.

The company even picked up some international publicity years ago when CBS golf commentator and six-time major champion Nick Faldo, who was in Akron for the Bridgestone Invitational at Firestone Country Club, made fun of golfer Jack Nicklaus on the air for chowing down on sauerkraut balls.

However, Kropp doesn't know where sauerkraut balls originated. "I don't think anybody does," he says with a laugh. Bunny B owner J. T. Salem started selling them commercially in 1964 when he founded the company, but it's unclear where the idea came from. Some people believe it's a German recipe. Others say it's Polish.

The company, believed to be the world's largest producer of sauerkraut balls, sells 3.5 million to 4 million a year. With a distribution area of only about 100 miles around Akron, that's a lot of sauerkraut balls being sold in the region. Of course, the company gets requests all the time from former Akron residents who live out of state and is happy to ship the frozen balls around the country. Those requests really heat up around the holidays, a favorite time to pull them out.

"It's not a party unless you're having a ball," Kropp jokes.

Schmidt's Bahama Mama

Schmidt's Sausage Haus and Restaurant | www.schmidthaus.com

WHAT TO DRINK WITH A BAHAMA MAMA:
The Schmidt's Bahama Mama is a spicy smoked sausage. What pairs well with spicy? Malty, of course. And Schmidt's Sausage Haus and Restaurant offers the perfect malty brew: **Schmidt's Dark**, also known as **Dark Force Lager**, a beer made by Elevator Brewing in Columbus.

Schmidt's Sausage Haus and Restaurant
240 E. Kossuth St.
Columbus, Ohio 43206
(614) 444-6808

GEOFF SCHMIDT pulls out an envelope from a drawer in his desk, opens it, and shows off the priceless, handwritten paper inside—the family recipe for the spices in the famous Schmidt's Bahama Mama. He figures that paper is from 1968 or so, the year after Schmidt's Sausage Haus and Restaurant opened in Columbus's German Village neighborhood.

He's willing to provide a glimpse of the recipe, but he's not about to hand it over. It's a family secret, of course.

Schmidt's has a long and storied past that dates back to its roots in 1886 as the J. Fred Schmidt Meat Packing House. That history includes an ownership stake in the city's professional football team, the Columbus Bullies, and the operation of the second-oldest concession at the Ohio State Fair.

But the company is probably best known for its Bahama Mama, a spicy smoked sausage that the *Columbus Dispatch* called the official food of Columbus. The sausage also attracted a visit by the Travel Channel show *Man v. Food*.

The recipe was developed in the meatpacking house and was brought over to the restaurant when it opened in 1967. The problem was nobody knew what to call the sausage. One of Schmidt's uncles, Grover Q.

Schmidt, was sort of a playboy who spent a lot of time in the Bahamas.

"It's always hot in the Bahamas and the girls down there . . . you know," Schmidt says with a laugh. "And he's a playboy. So somewhere along the way, in some kind of a meeting, and it's not really specific, they started talking about how hot it was in the Bahamas and with good-looking mamas down there."

The Bahama Mama was born. Schmidt finds it funny that when the German restaurant opened, none of the family thought to change the name.

Bahama Mama is a famous sausage produced by Schmidt's Sausage Haus and Restaurant in Columbus. The spicy sausage goes well with Schmidt's Dark, also known as Elevator Brewing's Dark Force Lager.

Think about it. The Bahama Mama is a fruity alcoholic drink. The name doesn't exactly scream German food. But, it works.

"It's not just because of the spice," Schmidt says. "It's because of the grind. It's because of the kind of meat we use. It's a beef-and-pork combination. A lot of people have smoked sausages, but I think they're a bigger grind and they don't have the same texture. They don't have the same bite that you get. The spice in a Bahama Mama doesn't burn you at the lips. It burns you at the back of the throat and comes back up."

Schmidt's also has had a lengthy—and, in one case, comical—relationship with beer over the years. The restaurant was the first one in Columbus to tap a keg of Michelob brewed at the local Anheuser-Busch brewery, which opened in 1968. That keg is mounted on the front of the restaurant.

There also was a famous old-line brewery called Schmidt's of Philadelphia. Many Columbus residents confused the two, believing that Schmidt's, the restaurant, also made Schmidt's, the beer.

Schmidt's, the restaurant, also considered opening its own brewery in the 1990s; they even went so far as to buy the equipment. The family ultimately decided not to enter the beer-making business. But today, the restaurant does feature two house beers, Schmidt's Dark and Schmidt's Gold, both made by Elevator Brewing in Columbus.

Stewed Tomatoes

The Pine Club | www.thepineclub.com

WHAT TO DRINK WITH STEWED TOMATOES:
If you've never had stewed tomatoes, you are in for a surprise. The dish has a thick consistency, much thicker than New England clam chowder. It also has a sweet, almost syrupy flavor. The **Warped Wing 10 Ton Stout**, with its roasted character, provides a great balance for the meal.

The Pine Club
1926 Brown St.
Dayton, Ohio 45409
(937) 228-5371

DAVID HULME isn't even sure how it happened. The Pine Club, an intimate 98-seat Dayton restaurant famous for its steaks, steak sauce, and salad dressings, and for its legendary stories—including how George H. W. and Barbara Bush were required to wait for a table just like everybody else—had been serving stewed tomatoes as its signature side dish every night since the place opened in 1947.

But around 2010 there was a mixup, and stewed tomatoes disappeared from the menu. They were still being served, mind you, but they weren't on the menu. Let's just say that longtime customers were not happy at all.

They couldn't imagine sitting down at the restaurant, so obsessed with tradition that the place looks nearly identical to the way it did on the day it opened, and not having stewed tomatoes with croutons served alongside their filet. The side dish quickly reappeared on the menu.

"A lot of people don't know what stewed tomatoes are," says Hulme, who bought The Pine Club in 1979. "They are such an important part of our culinary history in the Midwest and the South that's kind of been lost."

Stewed tomatoes, also known as tomato pudding, have been around since at least the 1820s. For many farmers, tomato

When The Pine Club in Dayton accidentally left its famous stewed tomatoes off the menu, customers weren't happy. The sweet, pudding-like dish pairs well with Warped Wing Brewing's 10 Ton Stout.

pudding was a special meal served with bread. The use of the word "pudding" is appropriate because stewed tomatoes are not thin, watery tomato soup.

The Pine Club believes its stewed tomatoes use the classic recipe. The restaurant takes beefsteak tomatoes and blanches them in boiling water for one minute. Then, the tomatoes are dunked in an ice bath, and their skins are removed.

Workers squish them by hand, then allow them to simmer in a pan over low heat for about 20 minutes, adding in butter, sugar, and cornstarch. Other recipes call for adding celery or bell peppers.

The Pine Club stewed tomatoes are thick with chunks of tomato and seeds. And, thanks to the sugar, they are super sweet, like a dessert.

Stewed tomatoes have proven so popular that Hulme opened a separate manufacturing site that produces 16-ounce jars of the side dish—along with the restaurant's house dressing and steak sauce—to be sold at grocery stores.

Hulme says he can't imagine a day when stewed tomatoes aren't on The Pine Club menu.

"You don't even consider that," he says with a laugh.

Tony Packo's Original Hot Dog

Tony Packo's | www.tonypacko.com

Tony Packo's
1902 Front St.
Toledo, Ohio 43605
(419) 691-8358

THERE ISN'T a more famous hot dog in Ohio than the Tony Packo's Original Hot Dog. Just ask Burt Reynolds or Wayne Gretzky or Howie Mandel or Danny Glover. Ask any one of the approximately 4,000 celebrities who have signed buns that are now on display in the five Toledo restaurants.

Or ask the fans of the long-running television show *M*A*S*H*, which featured the Toledo-obsessed Corporal Maxwell Klinger, played by real-life Toledo native Jamie Farr, who longed for the world's greatest Hungarian hot dogs.

Or ask astronaut Donald Thomas, a Cleveland native who took cans of Tony Packo's chili sauce aboard space shuttle *Columbia* in 1997 and cooked hot dogs—in space!

"That was pretty cool," says owner Tony Packo Jr., who has been working for the business since 1966.

The Tony Packo's story starts way back in the early 1900s when Hungarian immigrants in Toledo would serve a hot dog on rye bread for 10 cents. Tony Packo, a factory worker at the time, had a better and more economical idea. After he and his wife borrowed $100 and opened their own place in 1932, he decided to cut the Hungarian sausage into quarters, add mustard, onion, and sauce, and sell it for a nickel.

Perhaps there is no hot dog in Ohio as famous as Tony Packo's Original Hot Dog, thanks to its turn on the television show *M*A*S*H*. The hot dog goes well with Maumee Bay Brewing's Glass City Pale Ale.

That big fat smoked dog, a savory blend of beef and pork that comes either skinless or with a natural casing, was a huge hit with customers.

And just as Tony Packo did at the beginning, the restaurant still cuts the sausage in quarters. That's not to say if you want a big hot dog, you can't get one. Tony Packo's serves the M.O.A.D.—short for the Mother of All Dogs. It's the big dog unquartered.

Packo estimates that the restaurant sells nearly 1 million hot dogs a year.

But now, Tony Packo's serves much more than hot dogs. The restaurant offers a slew of Hungarian dishes, including stuffed cabbage and its signature chicken paprikas. It also packages many of its foods, including its chili sauce, pickles, and spicy ketchup, for retail sale.

The restaurant—filled with historical photos and other mementoes—had its first brush with celebrity in 1972 when Burt Reynolds, who was in town doing a play, stopped by and loved the place so much that he signed a hot dog bun as a memento. Thousands of celebrities have followed suit—although Tony Packo's has switched over to a Styrofoam bun instead of a real one. A few years after Reynolds signed the bun, the restaurant's name appeared on *M*A*S*H*, and its reputation as a tourist destination was sealed forever.

Packo laughs as he recounts stories of celebrities popping in over the years. Sometimes, the visitors are folks he didn't even know were still around, like the English rock band Uriah Heep.

But Packo, his eyes aglow with memories, treasures the stories of regular customers: the old man with a walker who talked about how his father brought him to the restaurant; the couple who had their first date there, or got engaged there, or even got married there.

Despite his passion for the restaurant and food, Packo has a difficult time explaining the popularity of Tony Packo's.

"It's not just one thing," he says while sitting at the restaurant downtown across the street from the Fifth Third Field baseball stadium. "It's the food quality, the level of service. It's something that you feel when you're here. And that's what resonates: the good times people associate with coming here, the smell. It's hard to put it into words."

INDEX